125

D0064726

7s. 6d.

POST-REFORMATION SPIRITUALITY

FAITH AND FACT BOOKS

CATHOLIC TRUTH IN THE SCIENTIFIC AGE

General Editor: Lancelot C. Sheppard

*This series is a survey of the Church's response to the challenge of
the twentieth century. One hundred and fifty books by scholars of
wide reputation, each an expert in the field he describes, will
cover the whole area of modern knowledge in the light of Catholic
teaching. Each volume, although a part of the overall encyclopedic
structure, is self-contained with its own list of references and
bibliography. The series is grouped in sections and the covers of
the books in each section are coloured uniformly for easy
reference.*

FAITH AND FACT BOOKS: 41

POST-REFORMATION SPIRITUALITY

by
LOUIS COGNET

LONDON
BURNS & OATES

This translation of De la Dévotion moderne à la Spiritualité française, *Volume 41 in the* Je sais-Je crois *series* (*Librairie Arthème Fayard, Paris*) *was made by*

P. J. HEPBURNE-SCOTT

Father Louis Cognet was born at Vichy in 1917 and was ordained in 1946. A Doctor of Theology, he teaches at the Collége de Juilly and lectures at the Institut Catholique in Paris. His published works include studies of the Jansenists and the religious history of seventeenth-century France and he has also written studies of Bach and Beethoven.

NIHIL OBSTAT: ADRIANUS VAN VLIET, S.T.D.
CENSOR DEPUTATUS
IMPRIMATUR: E. MORROGH BERNARD
VICARIUS GENERALIS
WESTMONASTERII: DIE XIII MAII MCMLIX

MADE AND PRINTED IN GREAT BRITAIN BY
WILLIAM CLOWES AND SONS, LIMITED, LONDON AND BECCLES FOR
BURNS OATES & WASHBOURNE LTD, 28 ASHLEY PLACE, LONDON, S.W.1

CONTENTS

INTRODUCTION

This book is in no sense a history of Christian spirituality in the classical period: restrictions of space would forbid any such claim. Nor does it profess to be a mere catalogue of names and summarized monographs. Its aim is less ambitious. In the last fifty years these questions have been the subject of much profound study and, in France especially, a whole group of scholars has striven to penetrate this hitherto almost unexplored field. But while some great works like those of M. Bremond or M. Pourrat are within comparatively easy reach, others are less accessible. There is need for a short synthesis, giving a summary account of the progress of studies so far achieved and providing an introduction to more specialized works. The aim of the present book, then, is simply to summarize the history and evolution of the spiritual ideas which led from the Renaissance to what is commonly called the French school. This means that, while its chronological and geographical bounds are clear enough, the limits of its subject-matter are much less clearly defined. The term "spiritual ideas" stands, in fact, for a very complex reality. They are not, strictly speaking, the speculations of theologians, yet ideas which seem to be purely theological often have profound effects on the most practical aspects of Christian life. Should we then say that our subject is the spiritual life as really lived by the faithful? But neither would this be quite accurate, for the idea includes social, moral, juridical and liturgical elements which do not come directly into our picture. What we are concerned with is both the thought and the conduct of the Christian, in so far as they form part of his devotion, his personal relations with God, his interior life—granting of course that the Christian must always be viewed in his proper milieu, the Church. Great religious personalities, of course, illustrious saints and the most approved theologians, are special cases deserving special analysis, because of their importance and significance. But they should never make us forget the milieu from which they sprang, and of which they are as it were the quintessence: it is the hidden life of the Church which we must try to discover in and through them. Only on these conditions can we fruitfully embark on a history of spirituality.

Up to this point I have purposely avoided the word "mysticism". This is not because mysticism is not one of the primary subjects of this book, but the word has acquired, in our time, so vague and nebulous a meaning that a definition is necessary before it can be used at all. We know that in the course of centuries this has varied considerably. At the present day almost everyone agrees with Dom Stolz that a certain inner experience of God and his action in the soul is an essential element in the mystic state. It is therefore mainly from the angle of experience of the divine that mysticism is here envisaged, bearing always in mind the problems raised by this definition, of which we shall have to speak in several places.

To attempt to give even an adequate bibliographical guide would be useless; the material is so abundant that this small book could not contain even a catalogue of it, and if references for every subject were to be given, interminable footnotes would be required with the only effect of making the text unreadable. At the end of the book will be found a Select Bibliography which contains only books that are easily available. Most of the books in this list will be found to contain bibliographical references which will enable the reader to supplement this short study.

CHAPTER I

SPIRITUALITY DURING THE RENAISSANCE AND THE REFORMATION

Christian piety at the dawn of the sixteenth century presented a very diversified appearance. It was a field in which as a rule there were no sharp breaks; changes took place almost imperceptibly, and time was needed to perceive them. The years which witnessed the enormous upheavals of the humanist Renaissance and the Protestant Reformation were very fertile in spirituality, but we should be mistaken if we expected to find any immediate or direct repercussion of these major events. Medieval tendencies actually continued for a long time, and new ideas were grafted into them without violence. In all problems of piety, personal religion and union with God, even the Reformers were fully conscious of preserving what was best in the Middle Ages and sometimes did not hesitate to espouse it openly. Luther, for example, is well known to have had a great esteem for the German mystics, whom he regarded as precursors; the praises he lavished on Tauler and the *Theologica Germanica* had the curious effect of causing works hitherto much admired to be suspected of heresy. First of all, therefore, we must study the survival into the sixteenth century of many of the positions characteristic of the later Middle Ages.

METHODICAL PRAYER; ST IGNATIUS AND THE EXERCISES

Nothing is more vague and inexact than the vocabulary of spirituality in the Middle Ages, and on this point a simple semantic study would be of inestimable value. In particular, such words as meditation and contemplation were given radically different meanings by different authors, and it is often difficult to delimit them exactly. There are no points of correspondence with our modern ways of thought. Nevertheless, from the fourteenth century onwards the more modern problem of mental prayer in the sense we now give it, the systematic and methodical practice of private prayer, began to be faced. The fact is that in the Middle Ages theology was erected into a speculative science and became separated from spirituality. Intellectual research came more and more to be considered a specialized activity, quite independent of prayer. Spirituality, on the other hand, was content with rather meagre speculative and dogmatic bases, so as to give more room for affective and imaginative elements. The divorce between them went so far that by the time of the *Imitation of Christ* intellectual interests were considered incompatible with prayer. In such conditions the notion of meditation was profoundly altered. Whereas the Victorines had once seen meditation as a real tension of the spirit, a conquest of the truth, now it became more and more an exercise of piety. This was an epoch of intense devotion to the life and human nature of Christ, which were constantly being put before devout Christians as matter for imitation. In such an atmosphere, the God-Man and his earthly life became the commonest subject of meditation, and naturally a method was sought which would make it easy of access to the great majority of Christians. In the milieu of the *Devotio moderna*, a form of affective and mystical piety which flourished in the Low Countries, this was a matter of intense interest. The works produced by the group of the Brethren of the Common

Life and the Canons Regular of Windesheim were of decisive importance in this connection, although in fact the whole of Christian Europe shared to some extent in the movement. First of all, they sought to provide the faithful with materials for their meditation, by regrouping the Gospel passages which would enable them to live anew the scene under consideration. Then some words of consideration were added, and thus emerged little collections of subjects, of which the Windesheim circle has left us many examples. Though this was somewhat earlier (about 1350), the great *Life of Jesus* by Ludolph the Carthusian was already widespread, and down to the seventeenth century it nourished many souls. Yet all this was not enough. Some had difficulty in developing the suggested subject by themselves, others wished to choose their themes more freely. Hence arose the idea of a formal scheme of meditation, applicable to any subject: the "method of prayer", in fact, made its appearance. During the second half of the fifteenth century Johann Wessel Gansfort published his *Scala meditatoria* ("Ladder of Meditation"), an interesting experiment in this field, but probably preceded by others of the same kind. Its tendencies led to an extremely complex method, in which the intellectual elements yield place to the imagination and the affections, and so to resolutions issuing from the will. Meditation thus conceived is both prayer and ascetic discipline. Such a conception must have answered to a profound desire on the part of the Christian people, for its circulation was very extensive both in the world and in the cloister. This attempt to organize private prayer achieved a decided advance at the beginning of the sixteenth century with Dom Garcia Ximenes de Cisneros, the Benedictine reformer of Montserrat, who produced his *Spiritual Exercises* in 1500. In these, prayer is used systematically as a technique of interior renewal, following a minutely described plan which leads the soul on towards a genuine form of contemplation.

But it was St Ignatius of Loyola (1491–1556) who brought this technique to its full perfection of form. The amazing success of the *Exercises* perhaps makes it harder for us in these days to guess what it was in this little book which was new to the spiritual world. We are not as well informed as we could wish about the origins of its various parts, but we know enough to state that we have here the fruit of a concrete and personal inner experience, and we might almost say that in some respects the *Exercises* are a work of autobiography.

We know that in 1522, at Manresa, St Ignatius began to take notes on his own interior life, and the essence of these is found in the *Exercises*. Though the question is still debated, it is probable that St Ignatius had read and followed out Cisneros and had borrowed some ideas from him. But it is not a question of external, literary dependence: if St Ignatius borrowed something from Cisneros, it was only so much as had happened in his own inner life. A certain hardening, due to the passage of time, is perhaps the reason why certain commentators are now unable to recognize as they should that the *Exercises* are drawn from experience, and recent controversies have shown that too often they were determined to see nothing in them but a mere manual of ascetics. It is clearly certain that St Ignatius drew from his own conversion a very advanced technique of interior renewal, in which ascetical procedures held an important place. This element of procedure is very striking. One feels that in the mind of the saint a series of acts, meditations and reflections, judiciously arranged, must lead the retreatant almost inevitably to a certain spiritual state—without discounting, of course, the action of grace, which could not be lacking to any soul of good will.

This technique is first and foremost psychological, and it seems certain that in order to construct it and bring its elements into play St Ignatius often had recourse to introspection. The procedure thus seems to depend quite as much on an exact knowledge of human nature as on the intrinsic demands of Christian dogma, so much so that it has sometimes been asked whether the Ignatian technique would not be just as valuable outside the context in which it is situated.

But the question is rather pointless, for St Ignatius never dreamt that this thought could exist outside the Christian context; further, more careful examination shows that it is just the fundamental elements of Christianity which have fashioned his thought, and that this is unintelligible without them. The *Exercises* are then a manual of renewal, of conversion, and it must be faced that only by a sort of extrapolation has it been possible to extract from them a complete spirituality, valid in isolation and sufficient of itself. But it is legitimate to do this if we endeavour to extract from the *Exercises* certain permanent lines of direction, and if we complete the scheme from the saint's other writings and his autobiography. The Ignatian spirituality thus obtained is extremely rich and flexible, and we shall not be surprised to find it strongly coloured with mysticism when we remember the mystical graces he received. In any case, the incredibly wide diffusion of the *Exercises* gave legitimacy once and for all to the idea of the "method of prayer". A great many of these methods were put out in the second half of the sixteenth century, but they almost all reproduced in one form or another the fundamental elements dear to St Ignatius: systematic use of the imaginative powers and the interior senses, deliberate incitement of the affections, ascetic and moral application. This combination of equilibrium and complexity tends to make mental prayer the supreme practice of piety, summing up and giving life to all other practices, though naturally without excluding them. By the end of the century practically all spiritual writers agreed on this point. This shows us to what an extent the influence of St Ignatius prolonged and developed one of the most important trends of medieval piety, right through the modern age.

THE EXTENSIONS OF MEDIEVAL MYSTICISM

Nothing is more striking than the importance of the mystical element in Christian piety from the fourteenth century onwards. It would of course be absurd to see it as a completely new beginning: we know that the mystical experience is as old as Christianity itself, and has its roots even in Judaism. But now we find a twofold phenomenon: on the one hand, the mystical forms of the inner life tend to become widespread, and on the other, the attention of the theorist is brought to bear on mysticism with lively intensity. This phenomenon has causes—moral, social and religious—which are too complex for us to think of analysing here. It appears sometimes in the form of a disquieting, even morbid effervescence.

Confining ourselves to the simplest facts, we can be certain that at the end of the Middle Ages, and specially in the milieu of the *Devotio moderna*, piety tended towards interior experience and ascribed great importance to individual psychological states; to be convinced of this we have only to open a book like the *Imitation*. This explains not only the prestige which surrounded so many mystics, but the success which followed the publication of their revelations. At the same time theoretical works abounded and were as eagerly welcomed. In this field, primacy belongs to what is called the Northern or Rheno-Flemish school. The condemnation incurred by Master Eckhart in 1329 limited the circulation of his books, but it seems that they continued to circulate in private, and that his ideas had more influence than is sometimes supposed. The works of Ruysbroeck, on the other hand, spread openly, and even the rather incomprehensible objections of Gerson did not check their progress. The same is true of Suso and Tauler. A little later the Northern school found its most coherent theorist and efficient propagandist in the Franciscan Hendrik Herp († 1477), better known by his Latin name of Harphius, whose works were henceforth in the hands of specialists everywhere.

The sixteenth century, far from renouncing this mystical heritage of the Middle Ages, lived by it to the letter and ensured its ever wider diffusion. Many of the Christian humanists were in fact sympathetic towards mysticism. Their fondness for it came no doubt from their attraction to Neo-platonism, with which northern mysticism is impregnated, and from the reading of the works of the Pseudo-Dionysius, whom the Middle Ages had never forgotten, but used with en-thusiasm. In the dawn of the century (1502) the learned Lefèvre of Étaples edited him with interesting scholia. So we shall not be surprised to find the same Lefèvre, a little later, in 1512, becoming the editor of a Latin version of Ruys-broeck's *Ornament of the Spiritual Espousals*. But the propa-gation of the Rhineland mystics was primarily the work of the Cologne Charterhouse of St Barbara, and it continued throughout the century. It was there that Bloomeven produced the *Mirror of Perfection* by Harphius in 1509, and from 1530 onwards publications increased at a surprising rate. Catherine of Siena and other Italians were added to the great names of the Northern school, and through the medium of Latin translations were spread throughout educated Europe. It is worthy of remark that the Cologne Charterhouse had close ties with the Ignatian milieu, and in 1543 the monks were even initiated to the *Exercises* by one of St Ignatius' first companions, a fact which clearly shows in what a mystical aspect the *Exercises* were already regarded. From every point of view the spiritual movement of the sixteenth century is greatly indebted to the Cologne Charterhouse.

This mysticism, which persisted thus throughout the cen-tury, remained faithful on the whole to the main current of the north. But the unity of this current should not be exag-gerated. Even if we ignore Eckhart's little-known ideas, notable differences are apparent between even the leading representatives of the Rhineland Flemings. It is typical of this, for example, that Harphius left some of Ruysbroeck's more daring themes in the background. Certain common features, however, are plainly seen, and especially the tendency to find the summit of the spiritual life in a direct, unmediated union between the human soul and the divine essence. This union naturally presumes the "by-passing"[1] (*dépassement*) of everything created, even of the humanity of Christ, which after all is a created thing. The soul attains to this by a complete spiritual nakedness, expressed in a rich vocabulary of annihilation[2]: self-abasement, extinction, nihility. This union with the divine, moreover, constitutes a stable condition, which Harphius, for example, expressed by the superlative term "superessential". As we can see, this was a matter of very general directions, leaving room for individual differences which would long remain, however, relatively unchanged.

In such conditions it was to be expected that the sixteenth century should see the appearance of the last great works of the Northern school, whose popularity showed how relevant they still remained. One of the best appeared in 1535 through the labours of Dom Thierry Loer, Vicar of the Cologne Charterhouse: this was the famous *Pearl of the Gospel*. It was an anonymous work, produced by some devout person living in the world, whose identity is unknown. It was written in Dutch, but in 1545 the indefatigable translator Laurence Surius, also a Carthusian of Cologne, made a Latin version of it which soon spread rapidly. Not only is the *Pearl* steeped in the themes dear to Rhenish mysticism, but in some respects it is a real anthology, for the author, or perhaps the editor, has not hesitated to insert entire chapters borrowed from other authors, especially Ruysbroeck. It is to the latter, on the whole, that the *Pearl* is faithful, but the influence of Harphius is evident.

While the author of the *Pearl*, like Harphius, admits that at the summit of the spiritual life it is necessary to "by-pass" the humanity of Christ, he gives a very considerable place to the mystery of the Incarnation and to the God-Man, who remains the sole way of access to the divinity. We know how

---

[1] This word is frequently used by the mystics to express the act of transcending, leaving behind, going beyond, all that is not God in order to come directly to the divine nature.

[2] "Annihilation" (*anéantissement*) is another technical term of the mystics meaning absorption without destruction.

important in medieval piety was the idea of the imitation of Christ. But the *Pearl* goes further and requires the Christian to be truly transformed into Jesus Christ, to form but one with him. The essence of this position is found also in Harphius, but here it is expressed with peculiar earnestness, in often graphic phrases. In this context the *Pearl* also adopts several of Ruysbroeck's ideas which Harphius had left in the shade, particularly the Neoplatonic theme of the "ideal being", the *esse ideale*. It is in fact a point dear to Ruysbroeck, and before him to Eckhart, to recall that from all eternity we exist in the thought of God, in the divine Idea, and that this Idea is at the very roots of our being, like an uncreated spark. To the author of the *Pearl*, as for his great precursors, the mystical life is a movement of introversion, by which the soul turns in on itself, to find that it is itself ideally uncreated in its bare essence, and so to be united in its centre to the divine image, by Jesus Christ who is its way. It is clear that the *Pearl* is at home in the most arduous aspects of northern mysticism, and we can understand why certain readers, like St Francis de Sales, accused it of excessive obscurity.

Not content with giving editions and translations to the devout, the Cologne Charterhouse also produced many original works. In the first rank of its authors must be named Lanspergius (1489–1539). Most of his work was done after the great shock of the Protestant Reformation, and is influenced by a very marked apologetic outlook. Lanspergius believed in fact that the most effective way of countering the spread of Protestantism was to revive the Church by giving the faithful a really fervent spiritual life. With this intention, eighty years before St Francis de Sales, Lanspergius strove to introduce the laity to devotion by means of his *Manual of the Christian Army* (1538), setting before all Christians an extremely austere ideal of self-denial, sustained by the example of Christ, and aiming at leading all souls to the practice of interior prayer, that is, of meditation. A great part of his work, however, is more strictly monastic, and shows us what

2—P.-R.S.

a solid intellectual and spiritual formation the Cologne Carthusians received. As he is aiming at reaching a comparatively
wide public, ascetic problems occupy a large place in his
writings, and he has purposely omitted the loftier flights of
Rhenish mysticism, familiar though they were to him. The
climate of his books reminds one in some ways of the *Devotio
moderna*, of Gerard Groot or Thomas à Kempis. Their
spiritual balance has won for them a lasting fame: in particular his *Discourse of Jesus Christ to the faithful soul* (1532)
was often translated and remained a classic till the seventeenth
century.

Wide as was the diffusion of Lanspergius's works, it was as
nothing to that of the Benedictine Louis de Blois, commonly
called Blosius, abbot of Lessies (1506–66), whose works were
later published by the Carthusians of Cologne. Notwithstanding some remote French origins, Blosius by his formation and
his tendencies belongs wholly to the Low Countries. Much of
his work consists of anthologies, collections of texts which reveal his spiritual tastes. The Fathers of the Church, especially
St Augustine and St Gregory, are found side by side with St
Gertrude, St Mechtilde and the great northern authors. Among
these he often quotes Ruysbroeck and Suso, but his chief
admiration is for Tauler, whose memory he is often bold to
defend. Though his work is primarily and mainly monastic,
written for the reform of his monks at Lessies, it has indirectly
in view the larger public of devout souls scattered throughout
the world. Blosius' own writings are usually rather short, but
highly concentrated in thought. His readers' needs oblige him
to devote a good deal of space to ascetic problems, but he is
anxious, even more than Lanspergius, to lead his disciples to
the heights of the mystical life. His views on contemplation
are much influenced by Harphius but owe much also to St
Gregory. He invites the soul to a mode of contemplation
which is bare of images, but observes that therein the divine
essence is never attained in itself. On the other hand, for him
as for Harphius, the summit of the unitive life is always

trinitarian: in a certain fashion the soul has part in the life of the divine persons. Moreover, Blosius describes this transforming union in very striking terms, reminiscent of Ruysbroeck. The little books of the abbot of Lessies, constantly translated into different languages, contributed powerfully to spreading the influence of the northern mystics throughout Christian Europe.

These few lines are far from providing a complete inventory of the survivals of Rhenish mysticism into the sixteenth century, but they suffice to show the importance of this current all through the Renaissance and into the classic period. Many of its works, in fact, continued to be read until the anti-mystical crisis at the end of the seventeenth century. One could quote, for example, the famous *Institutions* ascribed to Tauler. It is a compilation put together by St Peter Canisius before his entry into the Society of Jesus, and published among Tauler's works in 1543. Some of Tauler's texts are found in it, but Canisius has also borrowed from nearly all the great authors of the Northern school, and some of his sources are not yet definitely identified. Now as things turned out, this skilful anthology was long taken for an actual work of Tauler's, and of all the writings put out in the name of the great Dominican, this was the one most often published and translated. In it Canisius presents the teaching of this school in a simple, easily grasped form, arranged on a clear and balanced plan. Few works so well contributed to keeping alive the school's essential ideas, and well into the seventeenth century translations continued to appear.

THE RELIGION OF HUMANISM

While many of the spiritual ideas of the Middle Ages survived into the sixteenth century, the revolution in outlook provoked by the Renaissance was bound to have its effects in the realm of Christian devotion. The rediscovery of the ancient culture introduced men's minds to a point of view radically opposed to that which had prevailed in the medieval period.

In the Middle Ages the scale of values was based on an essentially religious criterion. The idea of God and the primacy of the divine prevailed unchallenged. Man was very highly esteemed, but that was because man is the image of God, and his chief end is to contemplate God in a blessed eternity. In spite of the progressive rise of national sentiment and of a certain anti-clericalism, the social organization was dominated by the idea of salvation. We can assert that in this respect medievalism was genuinely theocentric. In contrast, antiquity as revived by the humanists was an anthropocentric society, in which man had no other end than himself, no aim but the harmonious development of his potentialities. In many cases, we know, the love of antiquity did lead to real neo-paganism in thought and morals, and so to a more or less disguised enmity to Christianity, but on the whole such cases were exceptional. Many humanists remained sincerely attached to their Christian faith, while all the time trying to reconcile their religious convictions with their philosophical and literary positions.

The task was no easy one. The absolute nature of the divine primacy is not just a medieval position: it is clearly bound up with the very structure of Christianity and cannot be eliminated from it. Christian humanists therefore tried to find a compromise in the idea of man's nobility and dignity, an idea which they thought to be in some respects common to Christianity and to the ancient culture. But here there was obviously some degree of misapprehension, for this nobility of man is asserted in the name of quite different criteria on either side. They were thus led to a spiritualized and opti-mistic view of pagan antiquity. They tried to make a synthesis of its better elements in order to see it as a kind of prefigura-tion of Christianity: in such an atmosphere they were all but venerating Socrates, Plato and Virgil as real saints. In Chris-tianity, on the other hand, they did their best to minimize all resistance to nature, all submission of the reason, so as to give religion a humanized aspect, as far as that was possible. The folly of the cross was veiled in order to build up a sort of Christian wisdom, as close as possible to the wisdom of antiquity. In place of the dynamism which had inspired the Middle Ages in their aspirations to sanctity through conformity to the suffering Christ, the Renaissance offered the ideal of a balance between the human and the Christian, all finely parcelled out and qualified, too aristocratic ever to become a really popular religion. The Christian humanists were sincere in their desire to serve the Church, realizing better than others its deficiencies and need of reform, but the artificiality of their culture led them to seek escape in Utopias —it is no mere chance that the word is the title of a work of St Thomas More, one of the most attractive characters of the group.

The humanists believed they were only doing their duty in denouncing the frailties, abuses and scandals of medieval Christianity, with the aim of substituting for it a purified, rationalized religion. But they could not foresee that their criticisms would serve mainly to provide weapons for the Reformers, while the positive part of their programme remained inaccessible to the masses. At the dawn of the new age, the humanists looked forward with enthusiasm to the renewal of the religious climate. A typical example of this is John Pico della Mirandola (1463–94). In 1486 he published in Rome his nine hundred theses *In omni genere scientiarum* ("on all kinds of knowledge"), constituting a sort of *Summa* of humanist philosophy and theology; on certain points they were so daring that Innocent VII felt obliged to condemn thirteen of them. As an introduction to his theses, Pico had composed a *Discourse on the Dignity of Man*, in which he set out all the hopes of the Renaissance. In this he tried to justify his own position; he saw a harmony, a profound concord, between the wisdom of antiquity, the Cabbala or secret gnosis of the Jews, and the truths of Christianity. This was certainly the most daring syncretism yet proposed. There is little doubt that Pico della Mirandola later came to see the mistaken nature of his attempt: it appears that by the time of his premature death, and under the influence of Savonarola, he had renounced the mirage of human sciences.

But if we would see the very type of the Christian humanist, the obvious name is that of Erasmus (1467–1536). The cosmopolitan character of his career, the fame of his learning and writings, the universal diffusion of his religious thought, all combined to make him one of the most significant figures of the Renaissance. Now, on the plane of spirituality, he very early defined his position by the publication of his *Manual of the Christian Knight* (1504). In all his later work he only developed its essential ideas, abandoning none of them. He had a complex formation. The humanist strain in him was strong, but his youth was linked with the Brethren of the Common Life and with Windesheim, and so with the mystical piety of the Low Countries, a synthesis which partly explains the originality of his character. The *Manual* of Erasmus is not made for the many: it is addressed to the *élite* of educated Christians, and this limitation alone suffices to decide its bearing and gives us an idea of its weaknesses. In his fight against the devil and the world, the Christian knight has as his weapons prayer and knowledge. The manner in which Erasmus conceives of prayer reveals the influence of the *Devotio moderna*, for he is here concerned essentially with interior prayer, springing from the soul and the heart. The spiritual life, as he sees it, is discreetly but firmly opposed to the mass of outward practices which had flourished in the Middle Ages: he is ever ready to remind us that true piety does not consist in these. But he leaves the mystical aspects of this interior prayer in the background and establishes it first on the intellectual and rational plane. The kind of meditation he commends to his knight is formed chiefly of well-ordered considerations on the frailty of this present life, the reality of eternal rewards and the sufferings of Christ.

Here he is faithful to the spirit of the *Devotio moderna* in constantly recalling his reader to the imitation of Christ. As for the knowledge which is the Christian's other weapon, Erasmus sees this first and foremost as familiarity with the Holy Scriptures. Here, too, he centres his attention on the person of Christ, and the Gospels are in fact the prime object of his interest. An excellent Hellenist but an indifferent Hebraist, Erasmus devoted a considerable volume of exegesis to the New Testament, almost entirely neglecting the Old. But for the rest, the discovery of the literal sense is to him only an intermediate stage: what matters is the knowledge of the hidden, symbolic sense, and he draws his disciple on to the allegorical explanation. This explanation must not spring from unfettered fancy. There are of course many cases where there is nothing to decide the interpretation of the sacred books: the best thing then is to trust to the inward inspiration of the Holy Ghost. But very often the sense of a passage has been decided by tradition and the teaching authority of the Church, and in that case the knowledge of the sources is indispensable. On this point Erasmus denies all value to the empty, verbose ratiocinations of the schoolmen: we must return to the Fathers, with whom theology finds its full flowering in the Christian life.

By his need to live in Christ and to refer all things to him, as by his return to the most authentic forms of Christianity, Erasmus expresses the purest religion of humanism. But within this solid framework other viewpoints appear, which show him to be a man of the Renaissance. There is, for instance, his conviction that there is a real harmony between the morality of the Gospels and the best in that of antiquity. His *Colloquies* (1519) express his admiration for the great writers and thinkers of antiquity, in whom he almost sees, may we say, Christians before their time. His reforming zeal is shown by the vigour with which, in *The Praise of Folly* (1511), he stigmatizes the abuses which defile the Church, in particular the degradation of the regular clergy, the monks. It is true that Erasmus' antimonachism, which surprises us today, was already a common-place: we must remember that a little later, under Paul III, a commission of Cardinals proposed the extinction of all existing orders as irreformable. It was moreover a common theme even among the mystics: the grave Harphius remarks more than once that the vows of religion are of little account compared with interior perfection. *The Praise of Folly* is in fact one of a satirical type already generally accepted, of which the *Utopia* (1516) of St Thomas More, Erasmus' intimate friend, is another good example. The weakest point in his thought is undoubtedly his attitude to suffering, and especially to voluntary suffering, to mortification. In his meditation on the passion he sees it primarily as a theme for moral considerations and recoils in horror from the excessive preoccupation with pain so dear to medieval meditation. Here and there he speaks favourably of mortification, but for him the word seems to mean no more than the equilibrium of a soul which is master of its passions: the pursuit of a wisdom which is both human and Christian tends here to weaken the traditional demands of asceticism.

His ideal is indisputably noble and lofty, and this religion of the spirit was able to win the support of an intellectual and moral *élite*. This was the case in France, in particular, with what is called the Meaux group, dominated by the winning personalities of Briçonnet and Jacobus Faber, also known as Lefèvre d'Étaples. Unfortunately, it is all an artificial construction, with no deep roots in the actual mentality of Christian people, too refined and subtle to act on the masses. It is easy to see what advantage the Lutheran reformers could draw from the ideas put forth by the Christian humanists, but the brutal clarity and rather vulgar eloquence of Luther gave them an effectiveness which they wholly lacked in the writings of Erasmus. The latter had not desired this, and it was in perfect good faith that he fought against Lutheranism, whose beginnings he had regarded with some sympathy. The humanists must have departed this life convinced of their failure. In 1535 St Thomas More perished on the scaffold for refusing to follow Henry VIII in his religious deviations. The next year, 1536, saw the death of both Erasmus and Jacobus Faber: they left behind them a Christendom irremediably split by the Lutheran crisis, and at the same time Calvin was publishing his *Christian Institutes,* the prelude to further divisions. A few years later St Ignatius of Loyola was to found the Society of Jesus: we can well understand that this mystic who was also a man of action passed stern judgement on Erasmus' aspirations, which he no doubt regarded as perilous illusions.

CHAPTER II

THE PREPONDERANCE

OF SPAIN

By its political power and by its wealth of art and literature, Spain in many ways dominated the sixteenth century, and historians rightly call it the period of Spanish preponderance. It would have been natural for this wealth to extend to the spiritual realm, but for the history of mysticism, as we shall see, it does not provide us with all we might have expected. Spain was successful in sealing off the Lutheran infiltrations which occurred within her bounds, as everywhere else in Europe, and so was able to avoid the brunt of the Protestant Reformation. But she only did so at the cost of the Inquisition, whose suspicions and excessive severity checked the development of Spanish spirituality and prevented the appearance of masterpieces that would have been irreplaceable. But even so enough remains to assure for Spain a place in the front rank of Christian history.

MYSTICISM IN SPAIN

If to some extent Spain was able to remain on the fringe of the religious drama which fills the sixteenth century, she owed it to complex causes, including her geographical configuration and diverse political events, which it would take too long to analyse here. But it was only this exceptional situation which made the action of the Inquisition possible or effective, and so, comparatively sheltered from the blows which shook Renaissance Christianity, Spanish spirituality in this age appears, more than any other, to be in line with the Middle Ages, though it was not unaware, for all that, of the contemporary movement of ideas. The Spanish universities were numerous and flourishing and their finest minds were captivated by humanism. Thus when the ideas of Erasmus began to spread through Europe they found firm supporters in Spain. Nowhere else, indeed, did his thought penetrate so deeply. Spanish men of letters, as a body, were ungrudging in their admiration for this purified, balanced form of Christianity which aimed above all at inwardness. Nearly all the great centres gained by it, but all the evidence is that the movement was led by Alcala. In 1527 at Valladolid, conferences of theologians began to meet, charged with examining the new tendencies, and the professors of the university of Alcala were unanimous in defending Erasmus. The famous *Dialogue of Christian Doctrine* (1529) by Juan de Valdes, an energetic defence of Erasmus' positions, is connected with the same trends.

Parallel with the humanist movement there developed in Spain some very vigorous mystical tendencies, appearing at the beginning of the sixteenth century in the movement of the *Alumbrados* or Illuminists. Here, too, it is hard to analyse exactly the roots of this mysticism, which may be largely a racial trait. One is tempted to see in it a distant survival of Islamic mysticism: the case for this has more than once been put forward, but the proofs are insufficient. In the thirteenth century, in the time of Ramon Lull, the thought of Islam had certainly a powerful attraction for many souls. But what remained of this by the dawn of the sixteenth century? By that time it is very hard to prove clearly any influence of Moslem texts, and the traces which some claim to find among the *Alumbrados* are far from evident. On the other hand, we must not minimize the importance of the many conversions of Jews which took place at the beginning of the century. The

Inquisition owed its origin partly to the desire to test the sincerity of their conversion, and it is a striking fact that many of the Illuminists belonged to recently converted families. On this problem too there has been a desire to connect Jewish and Moslem thought and to combine them in a single current, but this seems very difficult to prove, and we must admit that in many respects the *milieu* of the Spanish Jews is little known. Still, it is almost certain that their entry into the Church reinforced the desire for an interior religion, free from the misuse of devotional practices, and served to intensify mystical tendencies. Now it was that the mysticism of the *Alumbrados* began to link up with the movement of Erasmus, in its aspect of a religion of inwardness and a reaction against excessive formalism. It was very common for the *Manual* of Erasmus, translated into Spanish in 1524, to be a regular bedside book for the majority of the Illuminists. These, moreover, divided into two groups, united by many common trends, but distinguished by a certain difference of attitude to the interior life. One group, known as the *Recogidos*, attached the highest importance to the notion of recollection. To them this term meant the effort by which the soul withdraws from itself and from everything created, to allow itself to be freely penetrated by the divine action, and this total oblivion of the created goes so far as to include the humanity of Christ. Here we recognize the "by-passing" theme, so dear to the Rhenish mystics.

It is also possible that Spain was very early influenced by the northern authors, especially Harphius, but on this point exact documentation is lacking. The second group of *Alumbrados* was formed of those called *Dejados*, who built their spirituality on the idea of self-abandonment. They too rejected all created things and strove to strip themselves of all knowledge and all images, but their aim was to reach a state of quietude in which the soul is perfectly abandoned to God and is joined to him in a total "unknowing" of itself, as of God. Here too we are struck by an undeniable connection with the Rheno-Flemish school.

Recogidos and *Dejados* were not strictly opposed to each other; they were rather two emphases, two slightly divergent directions. But in the course of years an evolution took place which accentuated the separation. The partisans of recollection were very largely of the religious orders, men deeply imbued with a solid spiritual tradition. Their efforts were directed to building up a technique of the interior life and mental prayer, so as to help souls along the path to total nakedness of spirit and union with God. Little by little, these became the "spiritual men", the men of experience, to whom St Teresa commends us. The supporters of abandonment, on the other hand, insisted more and more, sometimes imprudently, on the importance of interior inspiration and passivity. They thus aroused the suspicions of the Inquisition, and it was they who were commonly known, later on, under the name of *Alumbrados*.

Our information about them is unfortunately not as complete or exact as we could wish; on many points our chief source consists of the Inquisition's own records, on which, naturally, only limited reliance can be placed. We ought, however, to pay particular attention to the edict published in 1525 against the *Alumbrados* of Toledo by the Inquisitor-General Manriques, a relatively moderate man and inclined to favour the ideas of Erasmus. Though it is hard to say how far this edict reproduces the ideas actually professed in the group, it seems to describe its dominant tendencies accurately enough. Now without hesitation Manriques detected in the group views which he declared to be steeped in Lutheranism, in particular on justification by faith alone, on the worthlessness of external works, and on the illusory character of devotional practices. Everything points to the fact that these infiltrations were quite genuine, and that many *Alumbrados* were sympathetic to the first manifestations of the Lutheran reform. In the subsequent trials of the Illuminists the charge of concealed Lutheranism recurs repeatedly. At first this had only mild consequences but, after the death of Manriques in 1538, it was not long in sending suspects to the stake. Even Cardinal Carranza found himself detained more than sixteen years in the prisons of the Inquisition on an unfavourable report by his Dominican confrère Melchior Cano. After 1525 the anti-mystical reaction grew yearly more suspicious and more decided, and the Index of Valdès (1559) went the length of proscribing not only nearly all the Rheno-Flemish mystics but also the majority of vernacular books on spirituality, including the works of Luis de Granada and Juan de Avila. Under such conditions mysticism became esoteric; it was expressed in confidential works circulated privately, or not at all. Authors who might have produced very important works gave up writing on these dangerous subjects and sometimes even destroyed their manuscripts. On this count the Inquisition is to blame for irreparable losses.

As may be supposed, therefore, it is in the first decades of the century that we must look for the freest expressions of Spanish mysticism, and it is a pity that on the whole these years produced only rather minor authors. There are, for example, the writings of the Franciscan, Francisco de Osuna († 1540), who in 1527 produced his *Third Spiritual Alphabet*. This work is known to have been of great assistance to St Teresa, helping her to liberate her own interior life and guiding her to the prayer of recollection. Osuna's treatise provides, in fact, a real initiation to mysticism. The devout Franciscan certainly had connections with the circle of the *Alumbrados*, and in many ways he may himself be considered one, though perfectly orthodox. He belongs to the side of the *Recogidos* and clearly expounds the essence of their views on recollection. According to him, mystical prayer is approached by complete inactivity, imposed not only on the faculties of sense and the imagination but on the memory, the will and the understanding. In this way he sets in motion a complete technique of interior silence. In so far as the soul attains to this it must fix itself wholly and lovingly in God alone, in a sort of total concentration which may sometimes result in ecstasy. The *Third Alphabet* is both brilliant and readable, and we can well understand why St Teresa was so fond of it. None the less, Osuna's thought is not always as firm and coherent as we could wish. In spite of occasional warnings, it perhaps tends too much to let us think that mystical union is the outcome of a series of processes, through which it is almost infallibly reached. We can see why even Juan de Avila thought the publication of the *Third Alphabet* inopportune. The author, too, may have realized this danger; he hastened to publish his *First* and then *Second Alphabet*, which are more strictly ascetical, and so to put things in their due proportion. Though it is scarcely possible to identify in detail any definite borrowing, it is probable that Osuna owed some general dependence to the Rhenish mystics.

This is a certain fact in the case of another Franciscan, a simple lay-brother, Bernardino de Laredo (1482–1540). In 1535 he brought out his *Ascent of Mount Sion*, of which he made a second edition in 1538, corrected and improved. It has been proved that the differences between the two texts reveal the influence of Harphius, from whom Laredo borrows verbatim. The third part of the *Ascent* treats of strictly mystical prayer, and we are reminded that this too was useful to St Teresa. But from other points of view, St Teresa is opposed to Laredo's spirituality. His tendencies, in fact, are extremely abstract and attach great importance to the subject of "by-passing" creatures: this no doubt came to him from Osuna and the northern mystics. At the summit of the unitive life, he says, the soul must transcend meditation on the humanity of Christ in order to contemplate the divinity alone. He too insists on the necessity of the "sleep of the faculties", which is the indispensable condition of this contemplation. But, more than Osuna, he stresses the divine action, which alone enables the soul to reach it. Laredo's mysticism is expressed with a freedom which was not seen again for many long years, and in spite of some clumsiness and obvious defects it makes his book one of very great interest. To this list of Franciscans we should like to add the name of St Peter of Alcantara (1499–1562). But it seems that this great mystic, the friend and director of St Teresa, out of prudence or humility, refrained from expressing in his writings the essence of his ardent interior life: the few works attributed to him, especially the little *Treatise on Prayer and Meditation*, are really only abstracts of Luis de Granada.

Luis de Granada (1505–88) is one of the most illustrious representatives of the Spanish Dominican school. His work is voluminous and translations spread all over Europe. His profound spiritual culture and experience of interior ways promised great things, but unfortunately he was visibly hampered by fear of the Inquisition. His *Book of Prayer and Meditation* (1554) is justly celebrated. He presents subjects and methods of prayer which are really adapted to the needs of the ordinary Christian and are clearly inspired by Cisneros. The book is remarkable for its balance and penetration, and the method it suggests was often reproduced or imitated. But it is obvious that the author has prudently refrained from mentioning problems to do with mystical prayer. His work on the whole is almost entirely ascetical. In this field he produced two works of great value which have become classics: *The Sinner's Guide* and the *Memorial of the Christian Life*. It is sad that such a gifted writer could never show his true mettle. For the rest, though the Dominican Order counted in its ranks many spiritual men, three of whom (Bañez, Ibañez and Garcia de Toledo) had the signal honour of being St Teresa's confessors, it was subject to the despotic rule of the terrible Melchior Cano, who carried his anti-mystical prejudices to the point of mania. He is known to have made desperate efforts to obtain the condemnation of St Ignatius' *Exercises*, though they had been published in Rome in 1548 with the approval of the highest authorities.

The secular clergy were brilliantly represented in this movement by Blessed Juan de Avila, the apostle of Andalusia (1500–69). He was rightly held to be most experienced in interior ways, and what remains of his spiritual correspondence shows that his influence was widespread: St Teresa herself consulted him by letter and showed him the manuscript of her autobiography. It seems that he was a very great mystic who had known the highest states of unity, but in his writings he maintained the utmost prudence and never broached certain subjects on which he could have had much to say. It was even against his will that his *Exposition of the Verse Audi Filia* was published in 1556. What mysticism it contains is very restrained, firmly embedded in ascetical instructions and accompanied by stern warnings against the *Alumbrados* and the Lutherans. The method of prayer he advises, rather like that of Luis de Granada, is wholly centred on the contemplation of the life of Christ and includes scarcely any other subjects. All the evidence suggests that these pages, beautiful as they are, express only an elementary stage in the author's thought. Within his self-imposed limits Avila's spirituality is extremely rich and reveals a profound knowledge of scriptural and patristic sources: in particular he was a notable thinker on the priestly life. Popularized by numerous editions, incomplete though it was, Avila's work had an enormous influence.

The Augustinian Luis de Leon (1527–91) behaved less discreetly and suffered for it. A very harmless little exposition in Spanish of the *Song of Songs*, which he drew up for a nun in 1561, cost him five years (1672–6) in the prisons of the Inquisition. A little later (1583) he produced his admirable work called *The Names of Christ*, which on both the literary and the spiritual plane is a masterpiece in every way. Into this symbolical commentary on the names given our Lord in Scripture he inserts some discreet allusions to mystical prayer, but one can feel that he is refusing to stray on this dangerous ground. By the splendour of his style and the depth of his culture Luis de Leon was one of the greatest writers of his time and we can only lament the works of genius he might have produced if he had been free to express himself. But his inner life, at least, found expression in his splendid poems, which bear comparison with those of St John of the Cross. *The Names of Christ* met with striking success and won their author fame and glory, so that after some years he was chosen to edit the works of St Teresa, and was able to accomplish this delicate task in a manner which for that epoch was relatively satisfying.

Even in the Society of Jesus the problem of mysticism had to be faced somewhat acutely. Though the meaning and import of this incident have probably been exaggerated by some modern commentators, there was clearly a grave crisis, the details of which are not known to us as accurately as we could wish. St Ignatius himself is known to have aroused the suspicions of the Inquisition, but soon after this affair, in 1527, he left Spain, hardly ever to return. After 1540, when the Jesuits began to settle in Spain, the attacks were resumed, and we have already seen how fiercely Melchior Cano could wage war. The charge of Illuminism naturally loomed very large in this, and the superiors of the Society had to be very vigilant in regard to it. For the followers of St Ignatius the ideal was certainly a mixed life, composed of both action and contemplation. Contemplation readily took a mystical form with them; Fr Nadal, one of the saint's first companions, even thought that a certain share in the graces of prayer granted to the illustrious founder must extend to all the members of the Society. In the spiritual climate of Spain this aspect tended to develop with an emphasis perhaps too marked for the proper aims of the Order, and certainly dangerous with regard to the Inquisition. Thus among the responsible superiors a tendency arose to interpret the *Exercises* in a more strictly ascetical sense, less favourable to mystical prayer.

The difficulty crystallized around the famous Fr Balthazar Alvarez (1533–80), one of St Teresa's confessors for whom she certainly had the greatest esteem and affection. Fr Alvarez' writings are few, but his spiritual states are well known to us through the admirable biography by his disciple, Fr Luis de la

Puente. Fr Alvarez' spiritual teaching made much of the prayer of the simple presence of God, and it seems that some indiscretions of those he directed must have alarmed his superiors, for he was finally ordered to stick to the common ways. This measure was approved by the General of the Society, Everard Mercurian, who since 1575 had forbidden the Jesuits to read most of the Rhenish mystics, especially Tauler and Harphius. Still, we must not ascribe too absolute an importance to these measures taken to meet special circumstances. The influence of the northern mystics on Alvarez was a fact, but it did not stop with him and it appeared afresh when the coast was clearer.

The famous Alfonso Rodriguez, indeed (1538–1616), in his *Practice of Christian Perfection* (1609), reveals an obvious distrust of mystical prayer and confines himself to ascetical views, whose rigour has sometimes been exaggerated. The work of Rodriguez was moreover widely diffused and was long held to be one of the classical bases of Christian spirituality. On the other hand, Luis de la Puente (1554–1624) is there to attest the vitality of the mystical current among the Spanish Jesuits. A disciple of Alvarez, he became, as we have seen, his master's biographer and apologist (1612). He reproduced Alvarez' ideas in his own works, notably in his *Meditations* (1605) and his *Spiritual Guide* (1609), so often republished and translated. Mystical problems occupy a considerable place in his works. Taking the *Exercises* of St Ignatius as his point of departure, he certainly adds other less apparent sources, including the Rheno-Flemish mystics. Borrowing from the northern mystics is even more evident in the works of Iago Alvarez de Paz (1560–1620), but as he departed for Peru in 1584 he remains rather outside the main Spanish stream. His work is very prolix and written entirely in Latin. He quotes copiously from the Fathers, but does not hesitate to appeal to Thomas à Kempis, Ruysbroeck, Harphius and Blosius. The sum total of his works constitutes a vast general theory of the spiritual life, in which an excessive

classification by degrees gives an impression of great artificiality. But by distinguishing four degrees of prayer—meditation, affective prayer, beginners' contemplation and perfect
contemplation—he introduced a scheme which was often to
be repeated after him.

As we can see, these last authors bear witness to the
relative improvement in the situation for Spanish mystics in
the latter years of the sixteenth century. In 1583 Cardinal
Quiroga published an *Index* which was clearly more liberal
than that of 1559, and in 1599 Aquaviva, the General of the
Jesuits, promulgated a Directory which, without rescinding
Mercurian's decisions, allowed full liberty as to methods of
prayer. These conditions made possible the appearance of
works left unpublished by St Teresa and St John of the Cross,
the two greatest mystics of Spain.

ST TERESA OF AVILA (1515–82)

In the exceptional richness of her personality, St Teresa is
both profoundly attractive and profoundly baffling. A very
great mystic, she was at the same time a foundress, with a
firmly realistic common sense, and this apparent antinomy is
only the visible aspect of an intense inner complexity. If we
admit that the reformer of the Carmelites was indisputably a
saint and that her mission was providential, we have still to
face the problem, on the human level, of her temperament.
On this point, we must admit, the experts are still puzzled.
About the end of the nineteenth century there were some who
tried to ascribe her case to hysteria, and this interpretation
found credence even with some Catholics. Nowadays this
strikes us as very elementary, but then we no longer accept
the views then current about hysteria. On the other hand, we
cannot be quite satisfied with the over-simplified views of
authors who insist on minimizing the facts and depicting St
Teresa as perfectly healthy and spiritually integrated. The
progress now achieved in characterology and depth psycho-

logy makes us wish that the question could be studied by some competent and impartial specialist; unfortunately it is difficult to work only on documents four hundred years old. From all accounts, St Teresa's admirable balance was clearly the fruit of a conquest, the outcome of a struggle, in which the neuropathic elements of her temperament played a great part.

We could hardly interpret otherwise the serious illnesses which beset her youth and left their painful effects on her whole life. She told Fr Balthazar Alvarez about 1576 that she suffered continually from pain and infirmities and that her condition had been worse since she entered religion. Her entry into the Convent of the Incarnation and the victory she had to win over herself on this occasion caused a shock which had the effect of battering a nervous system already seriously shaken, and her mystical experiences played later a decisive part in the reconquest of her personality. But this was not effected without difficulty, and she had to pass through a long period of anguish, quite comprehensible, but entirely bound up, it seems, with her constitutional nervous weakness. She could only escape from it through her certainty of the divine presence and action within her, in fact by her intense consciousness of the Other. Whence the importance in her eyes of those psychological elements of her inner life which were of a nature to reinforce, or, if you will, to objectify this certainty. Such were her locutions and visions, which with her seem to have been nearly always imaginative and purely interior in character; there is no question of psycho-sensorial hallucinations, as some commentators would maintain. From the time of the serious illness which followed her entry into religion down to her first mystical experiences, St Teresa appeared to be comparatively hesitant or at least incapable of a real decision. Thereafter, on the contrary, the sentiment of being united to God himself and dependent on him in all things was manifest as a power which raised her above herself, overcame her doubts and made her capable of the most arduous enterprises. But it would probably be vain to try to describe more precisely the spiritual mechanism by which St Teresa corresponded to the graces she received; too many factors in the case are beyond our investigation.

Outside the foundations of the Reformed Carmelites, St Teresa's influence was spread mainly by her written works which, as we know, were entirely posthumous. The least mystical of her books, the *Way of Perfection*, came shyly to light in the year after her death, in 1583, but it was not till 1588 that the quasi-complete edition appeared, from the hands of Luis de Leon. As always happens, her works pose various critical problems, simplified by the existence of a fair number of autograph copies; in any case it does not appear that we have here to regret any really important loss or destruction. But we have had to wait till recently to possess an edition corresponding in every way with our modern standards.

It is difficult to determine the exact circumstances in which certain passages were composed, but the chronology of the major works seems to be firmly established, and their order gives us precious information on the evolution of St Teresa's interior states. The literary value of these works is enough to ensure their author a place in the first rank of Spanish writers, but more, their sum total constitutes one of the most precious documents left us by Christian mysticism. This is particularly the case with the four great works which followed each other in this order: the *Life, by herself* (first composed in 1562, revised and completed about 1565), the *Way of Perfection* (first composed in 1562–4, rewritten in 1569), the *Book of the Foundations* (written in three, or more probably four, stages, 1576–82) and *The Interior Castle* (1577). Together with many of the saint's letters which still survive, they make up an enthralling spiritual autobiography.

This autobiographical character of St Teresa's writings is most striking. The saint never had the least interest in the literary aspect: she took pen in hand only by necessity or under obedience, and usually in order to tell her story. The anecdotal aspect of events concerns her little: precision and memory are lacking, she is confused about dates and details, though she always tells her story exquisitely. But her interest is elsewhere; its real object is always the analysis of her interior states. Her autobiography is presented professedly in the *Foundations*, in the *Life* and in the *Relations* which supplement it, but it occupies as large a place in the works which are at first sight more objective. In spite of their deliberately impersonal form, the subject-matter is always her own experience. On this score St Teresa was a pioneer; she introduced into spiritual literature a new genre which had great success in the future. Here she differs from the medieval mystics and their revelations, for the most part ecstatic and noted down by admiring secretaries. Her position is equally different from that of the great Rhenish authors, whose vast constructions insert both their own experiences and the confidences made to them in a substratum of metaphysics.

For her part she simply tells her spiritual story, taking care to draw practical lessons from it which may help other souls. She does not start from any *a priori* conception of the interior life; she relates her own experiences, the graces she received, her hesitations, her resistances, her successes. From these she draws a certain number of practices and counsels which seem to her of universal value. In the degrees she assigns to her states of prayer it is vain to look for any logical order determined by some exact criterion. It is a simple process of presentation and to some extent a chronological succession; this explains the occasional lack of coherence between her different writings. Hence too her psychological insight. She is little concerned to discover the objective reality underlying her experiences: under this head she admits only the common foundations furnished by the Christian faith. To make up for this she analyses minutely the subjective data of her reactions, revealing remarkable gifts of introspection, but she obviously yields unconsciously to the temptation to envisage mysticism in an entirely psychological setting. Her sanctity as well as her genius make her pages of incomparable worth, as her readers soon discover. Thus she acclimatized the analytical and descriptive type of work among specialists of mystical theology, and contributed towards turning their researches to a psychological approach. Her influence in this sphere is very considerable.

The result of this psychological empiricism is that she finds in herself, in her own experiences, the source of her writings. Yet the self-taught character of her work has sometimes been exaggerated. She had read much, but confessed that she had remembered little. In point of fact the importance of her readings lies in the extent to which they influenced her life of prayer, and when we find some trace of them in her written work it is in a vital and concrete fashion. This is so, for example, with the influence over her of Osuna and Laredo. Nor should we minimize her debt to her directors, and especially the Jesuits; the firm clarity of the Ignatian teaching enabled them to understand and help her better than any others. It is sometimes maintained that her initiation to the *Exercises* of St Ignatius was of decisive importance in her evolution, by stimulating the release of interior locutions and visions. Nothing is less certain, and it is not even proved that she ever made the *Exercises*. It seems certain, however, that she knew and practised the method of meditation which depends on them; this technique, in which the use of the imagination plays a large part, must have strengthened what we might call her sensorialism, her tendency to objectify interiorly the graces received in her prayer, in the form of words and visions. Further, the Jesuits' counsels drew her to the contemplation of Christ, from which, under Laredo's influence, she had rather hung back. After this, she never varied on this point, and was always hostile to the idea of "by-passing". That she was opposed on this point to St John of the Cross is very likely. In every respect, Teresan mysticism is Christocentric.

In point of fact, what contrasts her with St John of the Cross is precisely her sensorialism. The way she offers us is certainly an interior way, in which the soul is invited to enter into itself in order to find God, but never does she accept the "nothing", the refusal, the fundamental negation of the interior world as well as the exterior. She strives to walk in the light, not in the night, and her path is one of supernatural knowledge, as clear and distinct as possible. In such an atmosphere we can well understand the value she placed on visions and interior locutions, which gave her strength in her worst sufferings. Nor does it surprise us that even her highest unitive states were accompanied by visual images, such as her transfixion by the seraph.

Some commentators have thought that here we meet with one of the limitations of her mysticism. There is no doubt that she enjoyed one of the deepest experiences of the ineffable ever granted to a human being, but the expression of it was often reduced by this sensorialism to a drama of images, which are perhaps rather misleading. It would be going too far to claim that for a theophany of the unformulated God she has substituted a theophany of the personal God of the Scriptures: on the contrary, the very structure of her experiences is bound up with the essence of Christian dogma, and so with the God of Revelation. But it can be rightly granted that to some extent she is enclosed in the world of images, so that she cannot find her way out: she lingers over the description of states which St John of the Cross surmounts at a bound. But we may perhaps be thankful for it, for this habit of hers has given us unique, unforgettable analyses, which have created one of the most perfect types of Christian mysticism. With the publication of Mother Teresa's writings, restricted though it was, a new period began in the history of spirituality.

St Teresa ascribes great importance to mental prayer, to which she believed her own conversion to be due. This practice was not then in use among the Calced Carmelites, and we do not know precisely under what conditions it was started. The part played by mental prayer in her interior evolution was such that in time she came practically to identify the spiritual life with the life of prayer. The degrees she assigns to it, in a somewhat clumsy and fluctuating manner, sum up naturally her own story. At the base she sets meditation, without providing any precise method, advising simply the consideration of the great Christian mysteries and the life of Christ, especially the passion. She notes that she herself has often found great help in the sight of creatures, of the country, water or flowers. On the other hand she admits that she is incapable of discoursing with the understanding: meditation as she conceives it is intellectually below the mediocre. From her own experience she has learnt the danger of a meditation so meanly conceived, a tedious repetition, producing dryness and disgust. The remedy she recommends at once constitutes, as she has no doubt, an approach to mystical forms. She recommends, in fact, that meditation be simplified by the use of an anti-intellectual and interior process, which makes it first an affective prayer and then a prayer of recollection. For her, however, the passage to strictly mystical prayer is absolutely gratuitous and depends on the divine intervention alone. Unlike St John of the Cross, she scarcely thinks it possible for human effort to prepare the soul for it. On the other hand, she so contradicts herself on this point that it is hard to say whether she believes all are called to mysticism, or that it is a favour reserved for some privileged souls.

Going on from meditation, St Teresa tries to classify what she considers mystical states of prayer, describing them with charming but rather prolix abundance. She mixes up terminology and degrees at her pleasure, so that over-scrupulous commentators have had to perform prodigies to supply the coherence she lacks. Recollection, quietude, all such things in fact, represent for her only steps on the path which leads to the sleep of the faculties, the indispensable condition of the divine union. On this point her experiences are clearly in agreement with the views of Osuna and Laredo; but, even more than they, she insists on the need for a special *3.* act of God to enable the soul to reach perfect recollection and interior silence. At this stage the soul is ready for God to introduce it to the unitive life.

In this life her experiences have led her to distinguish two levels. The first, which she sometimes calls the prayer of union, is characterized by alternating states of very diverse intensity, and the moments of union, in the strict sense, are *4.* sudden and transitory. Rather arbitrarily, it is at this point that she places the trials or passive purifications, and the extraordinary phenomena like ecstasy. Here her empiricism betrays her. Her exposition of the trials, though often poignant, is still superficial, for unlike St John of the Cross she does not succeed in making clear the organic bond which links these trials with the very substance of the mystical problem. In her analysis of the extraordinary phenomena, paranormal as we now tend to call them, she gives us magnificent descriptions of detail, but the total impression is indefinite and the vocabulary variable. In her thought, these exceptional graces prepare the soul for the supreme favour, the spiritual marriage.

This is the second and highest stage of the unitive life, transforming the soul and placing it in a permanent state. She connects her entry into this stage with a vision she had in 1572, when our Lord gave her the title of his spouse. Should we see in this the theopathic state, as it was later agreed to call it? No doubt we find the essence of it: inhabiting and total domination by the Other, capable of reaching the sense of fusion, even identification. Only, whereas for most of the *5.* mystics before her, the Other is the divinity, God in himself, for St Teresa it is Jesus Christ. Not that she is ignorant of this union with God alone: she notes that for her the spiritual marriage was preceded by a vision of the Trinity. But one feels that her need of concrete support led her at once to the more familiar theme of the Incarnation. In this degree of union, the soul acquires, as it were, a new personality, which enables it to give itself to an active and apostolic life, without thereby ceasing to taste God in its depths and to feel itself moved by him. Here, one feels, St Teresa is describing the state which was hers during the last years of her earthly life.

ST JOHN OF THE CROSS (1542–91)

Custom, chronology and their personal relations make it natural to compare St Teresa and St John of the Cross. None the less, when we pass from the works of the nun of Carmel to those of the friar, we feel we are entering quite a new world. It is true that when we approach St John we are bound to ask the preliminary question: how far do we know him? For his part he indulged in no personal confidences and left us no autobiography. We possess scarcely thirty of his letters, and they tell us nothing essential. These deficiencies are only inadequately made good by the depositions made in his beatification process. As for his works, we must admit that they are like a field full of ruins. What we call the *Ascent of Mount Carmel* and the *Dark Night* are surely fragments of one vast work. It has long been realized that the saint left this unfinished, but several experts are now inclined to think that there may well have been some voluntary destruction, demanded by reasons of prudence. The *Spiritual Canticle* has come down to us in three forms; if the first two are evidently the work of St John himself, the third, notably different from the others, has been the subject of impassioned debate among the learned, and the present tendency is to regard it as an interpolated rearrangement, made in the seventeenth century. Similarly, the *Living Flame of Love* exists in two redactions, both of which seem to be authentic. To these must be added a few short writings, several of which are of very doubtful authenticity. Of all these we possess practically no autograph manuscript, and the variants of the copies are often almost insoluble.

This deplorable state of affairs is explained by the precarious conditions in which the saint's works were written. We must accept the fact that all his writings before his imprisonment with the Calced Carmelites of Toledo in 1577 are certainly lost, since his papers were then seized. Though the dates of composition of his various works are much disputed, it seems that his period of intensest literary activity was during his stay at Granada, from 1582 to 1585. At the time the shadow of the Inquisition still lay dark over Spain and the mystics could not express themselves freely, so the saint's writings had to circulate under cover. He had besides to guard himself from the suspicions of the Calced. From 1588 onwards St John came into conflict with Nicholas Doria, whose views dangerously compromised the Teresan reform, and both his person and his works were suspect. It is from this time that some irreplaceable suppressions must be dated. After the saint's death his work was scarcely better treated. Regarded at first with some mistrust, it was not published till 1618, and then in a very incomplete fashion, since this impression does not include the *Canticle*. This edition, like all its successors till the present day, is cumbered with many alterations and interpolations which seriously disfigure the author's thought. It is only in our own day that an authentic text of the complete works has been published, but we still await a really satisfactory critical edition.

St John of the Cross expounds his mysticism on two different levels. First there are his magnificent poems, which set the humble Carmelite among the greatest poets of classical Spain. On this lyrical plane his interior life is expressed in a scheme of symbols, subtle and evocative, but very hard to decipher. Parallel with these, on the didactic plane, his speculative views on mystical theology are revealed by the commentary on three of the poems. This commentary's connection with the text is not always very natural. For the *Canticle* and the *Living Flame* he explains the succession of symbols fairly closely, but for the *Ascent* he follows the verses only remotely and they are hardly more than a pretext for a systematic treatise. The dry and almost scholastic form of the commentaries is apt to surprise the unprepared reader, and, interesting as they are, we may justly think that here we have a relative impoverishment of the lyrical expression. These poems associate St John with a literary genre exemplified by Garcilaso and Luis de Leon. At for the commentaries, their objectivity, their readiness to generalize and their systematic presentation put them in a class with Ruysbroeck and Harphius. But St John is still original by reason of his method, which is to take a lyrical text as the basis of a didactic treatise.

We have only to read the poems to see that they express a profound personal experience, and we know that several, including the *Canticle*, were composed during the tragic period of the Toledo prison. As for the commentaries, it is impossible to disentangle the autobiographical element: the saint has utilized not only his own experiences but those which others had confided to him, and recollections of his reading. This brings us to the problem of his sources, on which much ink has flowed without the emergence of any clear solution. The question is complicated by the fact that in the conditions under which he wrote he could hardly with safety quote anything but Scripture and some commonplaces of the schools. His temperament, too, led him to incorporate into his personal synthesis elements borrowed from his precursors, so that it is almost impossible to identify precisely what he has borrowed. Some have tried to trace connections between his mysticism and Islamic thought, but this remains a very tenuous hypothesis. Comparison with the northern authors, on the contrary, has produced very interesting results and merits further exploration. Everything leads us to conclude that the saint knew most of them through Latin translations, and while he was certainly much influenced by Tauler he was acquainted with Harphius and perhaps Ruysbroeck. From another quarter, he was clearly inspired by St Catherine of Genoa. Finally, like everyone else, he owed something to

the reading of Pseudo-Dionysius. As for the expressions and
schemas which he sometimes borrows from scholastic
theology, it would be unwise to exaggerate their importance
or to see in them any more than a concession to the habits
of his day. From another point of view, it may be asked
whether there is complete homogeneity between that great
work, obviously very abstract in tendency, called the *Ascent
of Mount Carmel*, and the Christological mysticism expressed
in the *Canticle* and the *Living Flame*. Some claim to see in
them two quite different lines of thought: it is more natural
to think that the second group expresses only a part of what
appeared in the great work, of which we possess, unfortunately, only these two fragments.

The mysticism of St John of the Cross is anti-intellectual, *non-conceptual*
or more strictly anti-notional. To be convinced of this one
has only to see what a low idea he has of meditation, how
poorly he esteems it, as merely a discursive act, produced by
means of forms and figures born of the imagination, from
which he banishes every trace of religious inquiry. In his eyes
it is an exercise for beginners, a mere technique of interior
concentration. It is desirable that the soul should pass beyond
this stage as soon as possible, and it will do so if it is faithful
to the grace which God never refuses to souls of good will.
This concentration has to take place before one can advance
further, and St John lays down very clear signs which mark
the call to the contemplative state; but he readily admits, like
St Teresa, that God sometimes dispenses certain souls from
the preliminaries, and they enter that state without delay. It
is from this level that the problem really begins to interest
him: his own doctrine is essentially contemplative, in the
sense in which contemplation transcends the ways of reasoning and dialectic. By his anti-intellectualism he joins hands
with the great tradition of mysticism which preceded him, but
he surpassed all others in giving it solid and coherent expression.

The fundamental reason for this is that his mysticism is

above all one of negation. The root of his system is the absolute refusal of everything created, as much in oneself as outside oneself; it is a nothing, *nada*. Where did he find this radical position? Without trying to transform St John of the Cross into a metaphysician, as has too often been done, it is difficult not to see in this a fundamental judgement of value. God is the Absolute and can have no common measure with anything created. Consequently no human knowledge, no notion of sense or intellect, is capable of really bringing us near to God. Therefore the only preparation which can lead to the mystical union is a negative activity of "annihilation": the soul can find God only by refusing everything created, refusing itself. With incredibly logical rigour St John states what objects must be subjected to this work of annihilation; it includes everything, up to the highest gifts in the supernatural order, supernatural favours, visions and interior words, and here we see how opposed St John is on this point to St Teresa. The soul must make void all its faculties, will, understanding and memory alike. What is here demanded is not merely the sleep of the powers, it is absolute emptiness, the desert.

In this vertiginous "naughting", this uncompromising world-denial, the saint goes farther than any before him. We do not find in him those magnificent insights, dear to the Rheno-Flemish mystics, on the continuity of the spiritual nature uniting the soul to God. His mysticism is one of introversion, in this sense that the soul has to turn in on itself and to turn itself away from the world around it. But for the northern authors it was by plumbing its own being to the depths that the soul found God in its centre; for St John it is by pressing despoliation, nakedness and poverty so far that it comes to be ignorant of itself. We cannot say that any one of these ideas is itself original, but what is original is the systematic way in which they are handled and pressed to their utmost consequences, to form what may be called the "naughting" of St John. There is something of Pseudo-Dionysius about it, but unlike Neoplatonism this attitude is not based on a metaphysical notion of Being. Like his precursors, St John readily admits that created being is nothing in comparison with the Being of God, who alone *is* in the full sense of the word. Yet he is little interested in this static "naughting" and his analysis applies chiefly to the dynamic "naughting", the voluntary annihilation of the whole notional life. Now on this point the presence of sin and concupiscence gives his ideas a very individual colour: in his eyes, the whole universe is stained by the Fall of man, and every contact with creatures involves a sort of impurity, up to the moment when the soul is perfectly united to God and finds things again in their original purity. Hence the need for a death of desire as well as of knowledge.

It was the same logic which led St John to construct his theory of passivity, one of the most original parts of his system. In his eyes, the negative effort of annihilation is the fruit of a grace which alone makes it possible; it is nonetheless a genuine activity, through which, he dares to say, a man can attain to contemplation. But experience and reflection led him to uncover the workings of the divine action more precisely. In fact, human effort, even aided by grace, cannot achieve this complete purification, which exceeds its normal powers of action. God himself must intervene to denude the soul, by an action to which it has only to submit and remain passive. But for him active and passive are not two successive stages. He was the first to formulate positively what others had only glimpsed before him, that active and passive are always concomitant. In other words he sees them as the obverse and reverse of the same reality. These passive purifications are wrought by God, through the sorrowful way of the trials, which detach the soul from creatures as from itself. So St John shows that these mystical trials are not something accidental but, on the contrary, an essentially given element of the path which leads to the divine union, and he has succeeded in constructing a really satisfactory theory of them on the level of argument.

4—P.-R.S.

This mysticism of negation is also one of darkness, which finds its natural expression in a symbolism of night: in this word "night" the mystical way, for him, is summed up. In a famous passage of the *Ascent*, he explains the triple sense he gives to it. It is a night by the total renunciation of the life of the senses, and this negation is a sort of night for all man's senses. It is a night through the path we choose, which is that of faith, dark to the understanding like the night. Lastly, it is a night as to the goal we seek, God himself, who in this life is a dark night for the soul. These phrases show how important to the saint is the notion of faith, considered as negation through its by-passing the reason. To his mind, the quality of darkness is of the very essence of faith, and he insists on its superdialectic and indefinable character, presupposing the renunciation of all human modes of knowledge and leading the soul to a notion, general and confused, of adherence to a Being who is above all formulation, all perception, all feeling —the spring whence one may drink only at night.

This plunging into the abyss of faith obviously implies "not-seeing", that is, a total rejection of images, and seems to involve even the "by-passing" of the humanity of Christ. Various passages seem to favour this interpretation, so much so that the seventeenth-century editors thought fit to correct them by interpolations. The pity is that in the mutilated condition in which the saint's thought has reached us it is impossible to be certain on this point. Some modern commentators have thought that he regarded the theopathic state as an experience of the Absolute, of a supra-dogmatic and almost pantheistic type. But this makes light of the authentic documents, which reveal that the saint's inner life was intensely Trinitarian and therefore bound up with the very substance of Christian dogma. On the other hand, the *Canticle* and the *Living Flame* seem to represent only the Christological and, dare we say, the Teresan stage of union: they do not exactly fill this gap. In the eighteenth century there were competent experts who observed that the saint had never spoken of union as accomplished by the universal and confused notion, that is, by faith. In other words, he had never developed the third sense he gives to the word "night". But from several indications we may venture to think that on this point he held a position we find outlined in the Rhenish mystics, notably in Harphius. Jesus is always the sole way to God, and it is in and through Christ that the mystical union is effected. The soul's effort towards annihilation must be accomplished by being united to the soul of Christ: at the end of the road it is by following the very movement of the soul of the God-Man that it transcends its humanity and is plunged in the divinity, to participate in the life of the three persons. This, at least, seems to be the line sketched in the last verses of the *Canticle*, and found, perhaps, at the end of the poem of the *Dark Night*. One is filled with regret at the thought of all St John of the Cross might have written on this subject, and perhaps did write, but which we shall never see.

THE ITALIAN SCHOOL

The glory of the Spanish school throws into the shade other spiritual groups which do not deserve to be forgotten. This is particularly so with the Italian school. Italy, permeated by every kind of influence, does not display the spiritual coherence of Spain. Intellectually, moreover, its greatest period had ended with the fourteenth century, which partly explains why the influence of Erasmus was there so superficial and that of Lutheranism so insignificant. In the philosophical and literary fields there gradually appeared a certain sclerosis, and also, no doubt, a certain exhaustion after producing so many masterpieces. Great religious figures lived in Italy, spoke, acted and shone by their example, but they did not write. Sixteenth-century Italy has left us no spiritual work which can be compared with the wealth of Spain in the same period. On the other hand, there were fervent groups in Italy, moved by the desire to reform the Church, to revive interior life and above all to inspire the clergy with a sense of their duties. These cares had haunted men's minds since the fifteenth century, but they became more intense after the shock of the Lutheran Reformation: they made a deep mark on Italian spirituality and were found even in those mystics who seemed most remote from the world. As a model of this type of Italian sanctity we may take the celebrated St Philip Neri (1515–94), founder of the Italian Oratory, who was the soul of the Catholic reforming movement in Rome. With a character which carried originality to the point of burlesque, and the heart of an apostle in its burning zeal, he was a director of the profoundest psychological insight and a mystic who reached the highest unitive states; he has left behind him an impression unique in the annals of hagiography, but he wrote nothing. The same is almost true of St Charles Borromeo (1538–84), in spite of the pastoral works published in his name. He was of sterner aspect, but his rôle as archbishop of Milan and in connection with the Council of Trent, his apostolic ardour and the austerity of his life, all combined to make him the very type of the reforming bishop, and in this capacity he exerted a powerful and lasting influence on the effort for the reform of the clergy. To his name should be added those of many founders and reformers of religious orders, whose holiness and labours were effective to the same end.

This zeal to recall the faithful to the Christian life was shown in the production of a great many works of an ascetic character, whose efflorescence marks Italian spirituality with a nuance all its own. They show a high development of psychology and moralism, and their esteem for human effort in the search for perfection is such that some phrases border on Pelagianism. This reproach was actually levelled against the author most typical of this tendency, the Dominican Giovanni Battista Carioni (1460–1527), better known as Baptist of Crema. The works of his disciple Serafino Aceto de Portis, or Serafino of Fermo, translated into Spanish and French, carried Crema's ideas far and wide and extended his influence. But the most representative work of the Italian ascetic school is quite a small book whose origins are still in many ways a mystery: the famous *Spiritual Combat*. When it appeared in 1589 over a *nom-de-plume* it contained only twenty-four chapters. Revised editions followed, corrected and ever more enlarged, bringing it up to sixty-six chapters. All these incarnations, whose critical history has yet to be written, lead us to suspect a plurality of authors. Its attribution to the Theatine Lorenzo Scupoli (1530–1618) is a tradition which seems to go back to the beginning of the seventeenth century, but it lacks proof. Other names have been suggested, especially that of the Jesuit Achille Gagliardi (1537–1607), a highly esteemed spiritual director; certainly Ignatian influence can often be seen in the *Spiritual Combat*. On the other hand, its interior asceticism is developed in a fairly original manner, especially as regards the good use of the human faculties. To us in these days, however, its psychology seems a little elementary, its spirituality rather thin, and we find it hard to account for the prodigious and lasting success of this little work, though this may be partly due to the praises bestowed on it by St Francis de Sales. It is also true that the tendencies to psychological asceticism only grew stronger all through the seventeenth century.

Parallel with this current, sixteenth-century Italy made an important contribution to the history of mysticism. She produced no great systematic work comparable to that of Laredo, still less to that of St John of the Cross. On the whole, the Italian mystics continued to belong to the ecstatic type so common in the Middle Ages. This phenomenon is easily explained when we remember the dominance still exerted over Italian piety by the person of St Catherine of Siena. In the eyes of many spiritual persons, she remained without question the very type of sanctity. It is in this atmosphere that we must understand that work of sixteenth-century Christianity which was destined to have the widest popularity: the writings of St Catherine of Genoa (1447–1510).

Catherine died at the dawn of our period, but in fact her influence continued to be very marked throughout two centuries, especially after 1551, when her biography and the works attributed to her first appeared. She did not write these works herself, and the essence of them seems to have come from notes taken down during her ecstasies. The composition of the whole has been attributed to her disciple Battista Vernazza (1497–1587), herself a spiritual writer of great worth, but it seems that in reality the matter is more complex and that the saint's confessors played an important part in this. St Catherine's work is wonderfully rich, and it is easy to understand the success which makes it still one of the classics of Christian literature. Her wonderful *Treatise on Purgatory* compares the state of the souls in purgatory to the trials of the mystical life: suffering there arises from incompatibility between the soul's impurity and the absoluteness of the divine essence. On this point the saint's ideas certainly had some influence on St John of the Cross. Though our Lord holds a very large place in Catherine's piety, she regards the term of the spiritual life as union with the divine essence itself. She sees this union as an identification of love which, to take effect, presupposes pure love in the soul; that is, perfectly disinterested charity, by which God is loved for himself alone, independently of his gifts, and in which the soul completely forgets itself. In this point her doctrine has a firmness and coherence which later on delighted Fénelon.

From the sixteenth century onwards her very personal mysticism inspired numerous works, especially the *Summary of Christian Perfection*; this little work from the hands of the Milanese Isabella Bellinzaga, under the direction of Fr Gagliardi, must have been written about 1584 and was probably first published in a French translation. Following a scheme perfectly in accord with St Catherine's ideas, but no doubt owing something to the northern authors, union with God is presented from the voluntarist angle, as a union of the human and divine wills, culminating in a real identification, in which the passive aspect is strongly emphasized. The *Summary* in its turn was to be the inspiration of many authors.

Certain traits typical of Italian spirituality are still more clearly displayed by some other mystics. Mention must here be made of the Carmelite nun, St Mary Magdalen dei Pazzi (1566–1607), who likewise exerted her influence all through the seventeenth century, and the Dominican St Catherine dei Ricci (1522–90). They show to what an extent mysticism was concerned with reform, in this being faithful to the example of St Catherine of Siena: both wrote innumerable letters on this subject to high ecclesiastics, who did not always in fact receive them. They illustrate, too, one of the profoundest characteristics of the Italian genius, what we might call their cosmism, their tendency to aspire to God through the contemplation of creation and its wonders. At this same time we can see an example of it in the purely ascetic work of the Jesuit, St Robert Bellarmine (1542–1641), and specially in his *Ascent of the Soul to God by the Ladder of Creatures*. The work of St Catherine of Genoa contains some magnificent pages on creation, somewhat abstract, it is true, in complexion. But all this flowers with wonderful poetry in the ecstasies of St Mary Magdalen dei Pazzi. In many Italian writers we may also note a relatively optimistic view of human nature, very apparent, for example, in the works of St Catherine dei Ricci.

CHAPTER III

THE REVIVAL OF
MYSTICISM IN FRANCE

So far France has played a very small part in our story. But French Catholicism, though its situation was complicated in many ways, displayed remarkable vitality in the sixteenth century. After some dark days it survived the crisis of the Protestant Reformation, and Calvinism gained only a limited foothold in France. On the other hand, the moral and intellectual decadence which affected the majority of the clergy and the faithful is an undeniable fact which must not be minimized. The enormous wealth of the Church of France—certainly more than a third of the national patrimony—was a prey which the commendatory system (benefices bestowed in *commendam*) too often put in unworthy hands. Church benefices were bestowed not only on courtiers but on children of two years old like Henry of Guise, who had six abbeys, or on Protestants like Sully, who had four. At the end of the sixteenth century more than forty bishoprics were held by laymen. Most of the bishops, too, were courtiers, diplomats, men of letters or soldiers, and never set foot in their dioceses. The country clergy were sunk in penury, ignorance, concubinage and drunkenness. Many monasteries were more like houses of ill-fame than religious houses, and the Fair Gabrielle herself blushed at the conduct of her sister Angélique, abbess of Maubuisson.

There is no need to dwell on this sombre picture, but it is essential to bear it in mind in order to establish the background of the spiritual movement in our period. For in spite of this generally low level, there were still in France many souls who were able to guard themselves from the surrounding corruption and to remain enamoured of perfection. Here and there their presence can be observed: the surprising output of devout literature in French, all through the sixteenth century, shows that books of devotion were finding readers in France, and this abundant production was barely halted for a time by the wars of religion. We must not then be deceived by the apparent desolation. Behind the abuses and the scandals devotion lived on and awaited its hour: not only politically but spiritually, the preponderance of Spain was soon to give way to the preponderance of France.

THE ABSTRACT SCHOOL: BENET OF CANFIELD
(1562–1610)

The troubles which so long divided religious France are no doubt enough to explain the fact that spirituality there remained more or less underground. Throughout this period piety was still trying to find itself and living by importations. Among the many volumes of all sizes which year by year continued to supply the religious market, there were occasionally some original productions, but they were of very slight interest. The plethoric work of the Dominican Pierre Doré, the Master Doribus of Rabelais, does not live up to the promise of its ludicrous titles, *Matches of the Divine Fire*, or *The Turtle-Dove of Widowhood*. But in compensation for this, foreign works, especially those of the Northern school, came to fill the library shelves, in the fine Latin translations of the Cologne Charterhouse, alongside the works of Pseudo-Dionysius, the favourite reading of spiritual persons in France. Then we must not forget that at this time nearly everyone understood Spanish and Italian. Very soon too, a mass of translations came to provide food for the devotion of pious Christians. In this abundance there was something of all sorts, but the best was represented. For the Rheno-Flemish mystics, Harphius appeared in 1549, but from 1553 the lion's share went to Blosius. Only in the early years of the seventeenth century did the greater works appear: the *Pearl of the Gospel* in 1602, and in 1606 Ruysbroeck's *Ornament of the Spiritual Espousals*, the French versions of which were made by the Carthusian Dom Beaucousin. A little later, in 1607, the Jesuit Jean-Baptiste de Machault (1591–1640) provided a complete translation of Harphius. It was much the same with the Spaniards. From 1572 several writings of Luis de Granada began to appear in French, and in 1586 Juan de Avila received this honour, not yet accorded to Osuna or Laredo. But it was not till 1601 that St Teresa was translated by Brétigny, who had already contributed financially to the publication of her works in Spain. A French version of the first works of St John of the Cross was made in 1621 by another friend of the Carmelites, René Gaultier, who in the next year translated the *Spiritual Canticle* while it was still unpublished in Spanish. The Italian writers, though they arrived later, were as well served: the *Spiritual Combat* in 1595 and the *Life and Works of St Catherine of Genoa* in 1598, both translated by the Carthusians of Bourgfontaine: their popularity was proved by numerous new editions. Then came the *Summary of Perfection* in 1599, and in 1600 the *Practice of Mental Prayer and Contemplation* by the Capuchin Mattia Bellintani da Salo.

These titles and dates give a good idea of the mystical tendencies in devout French circles in the latter half of the sixteenth century. They were accompanied by a passionate and sometimes morbid taste for the extraordinary phenomena of the mystical life—ecstasies, revelations and visions; diabolic possession, too, aroused lively interest. In such conditions numerous ecstatics appeared in all quarters, often among very humble folk, and almost all found secretaries to record their revelations. Typical of this class was Marie Teyssonnier, known as Marie de Valence (1570–1648), whom even the king's confessor, the famous Fr Coton, did not scorn to consult. We possess her *Interrogations to Creatures*, very marked in its cosmism, showing the Italian influence. Among all these mystics there was one who was to prove of quite special importance, becoming the centre of the devout circles of Paris: the celebrated Mme Acarie (1566–1618), who was the moving spirit in the introduction of the Teresian Carmelites to France, and died as a Carmelite at Pontoise under the name of Marie de l'Incarnation. Her very individual mysticism is quite steeped in the outlook of the Rhenish Flemings, and the few works of devotion she has left us are largely adaptations of Blosius. Her ecstasies and the other extraordinary phenomena of her life, with the influence of her outstanding holiness, helped to gather round her a group of spiritual persons. They included Capuchins like Benet of Canfield or Archangel of Pembroke, a Carthusian like Dom Beaucousin, without question the most renowned director of his time in Paris, a Sorbonne professor like André Duval, a Jesuit like Fr Coton, devout secular priests like Gallemant or Brétigny, who contributed with all their might to the establishment of the Carmelites, the young Bérulle, still seeking his true way, and layfolk like the future Chancellor de Marillac or the Marquise de Maignelay.

This group, by its deep and widespread activity and by its many pious and charitable foundations spread throughout France, was truly the starting-point of a movement, the origin of that religious spring which revived French Catholicism in the early years of the seventeenth century. It was therefore quite naturally the source of a spiritual stream which flowed through the century. The piety of this group was definitely mystical in character, and we have seen from its reading what was the source of its inspiration, in particular Pseudo-Dionysius, the Rhenish Flemings and St Catherine of Genoa. From these it derived a synthesis which, without being very original, laid great stress on the abstract side of this mysticism of essences. In this trend Christ is always the sole way of access to God, but the negative aspect of this way is emphasized, always seen under the aspect of annihilation. This annihilation presupposes not only the rejection of all created things but even the extinction of all conscious activity of the soul, in the domain of the senses as in those of the understanding and the will. Such a way of negation must lead to a direct, unmediated union with the divine essence, which involves "by-passing" the humanity of Christ, and takes place above the level of notions and concepts. It is attained by a fusion of the human will in the divine, resulting in a sort of depersonalization. This group thus earned the name of the abstract school.

Not many members of the group were spiritual authors. Duval wrote an admirable and strongly revealing biography of Mme Acarie (1621) and even his Sorbonne lectures show signs of the influence of the northern mystics. We have seen that they were translated by Dom Beaucousin: as Bérulle's director he had written for his young disciple a very abstract adaptation of Isabella Bellinzaga's *Summary of Perfection*, which was printed in 1597 with the title: *A Brief Discourse on Interior Abnegation*. The most noteworthy theorist of the group was the English Capuchin Benet of Canfield (1562–1610). It was only in 1609 that he published in France his *Rule of Perfection*, "containing a Brief and Perspicuous Abridgement of the whole spiritual life, reduced to the only point of the Will of God". The English version had already appeared, and the work seems to have been written before 1592. Canfield only lacks style to be one of our greatest spiritual writers, but in spite of clumsy and inaccurate language the *Rule of Perfection* was read all through the seventeenth century, and all the mysticism of the age was nurtured on it.

Canfield's work is an extremely advanced systematization of voluntarism: the whole problem for him is how to reach perfect conformity of the human will with the divine. He distinguishes three wills of God. First, there is the external will of God, signified in Revelation and in the hierarchy and discipline of the Church. Conformity to this external will corresponds to the Christian's active life. Next, there is his interior will, made known by the graces, motions and illuminations with which God favours the soul: if the soul is faithful to this it enters the contemplative life. Finally there is his essential life, so called because it is indistinguishable from the divine essence and is God himself. The soul which attains to perfect conformity with this will enters on a life of union with God, of transformation into God, which Canfield calls the supereminent life and describes as deiform. Imaginative and discursive meditation he regards as a mere point of departure and invites the soul to strip itself of all images and forms in order to reach a contemplation which is superrational and superdialectic. His fundamental thesis is that there is no proportion between man's faculties and the divine essence. There can therefore be no question of using the understanding in order to reach God, nor even of imagining any middle term where this union could be effected: the essential divine will must transform the human will by absorbing it into itself. While man has to make the effort to be annihilated and reach contemplation, his entry on the supereminent life is no less dependent on God's initiative: it is thus that the idea of the way of negation and that of passivity finds place in Canfield's system. He distinguishes, in fact, between active annihilation, the fruit of human activity, and passive annihilation, in which God alone acts. This latter is absolutely indispensable, and for the soul which is faithful to grace it always accompanies the active. At the end of this path the soul arrives at deiformity, a permanent and stable theopathic state, and Canfield gives an excellent description of its characteristics: simplicity, continuity, a consciousness of fusion and depersonalization. At this stage the mystic recovers full freedom of action, but his actions become those of the Other, who possesses him wholly.

The trend of Canfield's thought obviously presumes that for this unmediated union to be realized the humanity of Christ must be by-passed, and the original edition of the *Rule* was very positive in this sense, but the audacity of this thesis inevitably alarmed the Capuchin superiors, and when the "official" edition of 1610 appeared six chapters on the contemplation of the Passion were added to the end of the third part, which treats of the supereminent life, and several phrases considered too rash were corrected. On many points one is struck by a surprising correspondence with St John of the Cross, though Canfield cannot have known him. They agree in toning down the Platonic themes of their Rhenish precursors on the presence of the uncreated God in the soul's centre; but the Capuchin has perhaps gone further than the Carmelite in systematizing his construction. To the sources common to the whole abstract school Canfield adds, on some points, a contribution of his own, which he was certainly the only man in France to use: that of the English mystics of the fourteenth century, especially Walter Hilton's *Scale of Perfection* and the remarkable anonymous work called the *Cloud of Unknowing*. By the individuality and coherence of his synthesis Canfield, although he was an Englishman, remains one of the great names of French spiritual history, and it is a thousand pities that he could not write.

ST FRANCIS DE SALES (1567–1622) AND HIS FIRST DISCIPLES

In spite of its apostolic outlook, the abstract school lived by an ideal of mysticism accessible only to a very limited number. The task of transforming monastic devotion into popular devotion, of bringing the piety of the cloister into the world, fell to another representative of the Counter-Reformation. St Francis de Sales, though a native of Savoy, owed much of his formation to the Parisian *milieu*. From his brilliant studies he derived a strong strain of humanism. In another direction he frequented the entourage of Mme Acarie. But he was not at first attracted by mysticism. The conditions of the diocese of Geneva forced him, more than others, to face the problem of the Calvinist Reformation. His peculiar merit was to understand that the court apologists, like Cardinal Perron, could solve nothing by accumulating texts and that the real battle had to be fought out elsewhere, on the field of Christian life. He saw that many souls were drawn to Calvinism in the hope of finding in it a personal, interior religion, together with a perfectly worthy moral life, free from the formalism which too often vitiated Catholic piety. Hence the need to guide ordinary Christians to a sincere and fervent interior life, penetrating the whole of their conduct. The idea was not new. A few months before the *Introduction* of St Francis de Sales, Fr Coton published his *Interior Occupation of a Devout Soul*, to teach the courtiers how to sanctify even their least actions. But St Francis attacked the problem nearer its source and more coherently.

When in 1608 he published his *Introduction to the Devout Life* he condensed in it the fruits of a long experience of souls. By the word "devotion" he means an integral Christianity, involving the whole life of the believer, whatever his place in society: he wants to show Christians that the whole stuff of their existence must be steeped in the religion to which they belong, so that their life will match their external profession of Catholicism. So the saint does not shrink from coming down to the concrete, psychological level to explain in detail how this ideal can be realized: these aims give the *Introduction* an animated character which is enhanced by the charm of his style. At this stage he is concerned to attract as many persons as possible to devotion, which he ingeniously presents in an optimistic, human and irresistible manner. On these levels he has nothing to do with mysticism, still less with the abstract school, for which he openly shows his distrust. The method of prayer he recommends to Philothea is entirely imaginative and dialectic: the obvious borrowings from Luis de Granada are perhaps mixed with some Ignatian recollections.

The *Introduction* itself reveals St Francis as the director of souls, and we can complete the portrait from his correspondence and the confidences of his disciples. Direction was truly the passion of his life. To grasp the particular state of each soul he brought to bear an insatiable curiosity and an ever vigilant penetration. On the model of the Italian school, he gave an important place in his spirituality to the moral and psychological factors. In his search for practical solutions he showed a flexibility and adaptability which have sometimes been looked down on as a sort of soft condescension. But such a view of Salesian "sweetness" is an illusion born of misunderstanding. His penitents were unanimous in saying that he led souls by austere paths and did not hesitate to cut to the quick; but he could always do so with profound understanding of the human elements. Direction of conscience existed, of course, long before St Francis, but he transformed the factors of the problem, and his psychological approach started a current which prolonged his influence all through the history of Christian spirituality.

It was precisely his practice of direction which led him to modify his ideas on many points, and in particular on mysticism. In 1604, when he first came to know the Baroness de Chantal, she had already experienced contemplative states for some time. At first his direction was too purely ascetic and moral to satisfy her needs; whence the slight uneasiness in their relations at that time. Accordingly in 1606 Mme de Chantal got into touch with the Carmelite Sisters who had just settled in Dijon. Through them she was initiated to the ideas of the abstract school, and was naturally advised to give up the imaginative and conceptual forms of meditation. St Francis was at first very reserved about it; then he came to accept the point of view and even, later, to adopt it for his own use. He read mystical authors, whom so far he had neglected; he reflected, and the experiences of Mme de

Chantal and the first Visitation Sisters offered him an excellent field for observation. A whole new world opened to him. Step by step he tried to group and arrange his ideas on this point, and the result was the *Treatise on the Love of God* (1616).

The *Treatise* is a very complex work, combining varied influences in a very original synthesis. The voluntarism of St Francis de Sales here joins hands to some extent with that of Canfield. For him, as for most authors of his time, love has its seat in the will: it is then a matter, there too, of attaining a perfect conformity of the human will with the divine. But in contrast with Canfield he develops the psychological aspect of this scheme much more than the metaphysical. His optimism, born of his humanist education, impels him to find a certain orientation towards God in the human will, even after the original Fall. Our faculties of knowing and loving continue to have God for their object, and this gives supernatural charity the foundation of a natural love for God, and creates between God and man a sort of spontaneous contemplative relation. St Francis is careful, of course, not to fall into Pelagianism: he holds, in fact, that concupiscence, the result of original sin, makes it impossible for man to exercise his fundamental potentialities without grace. It cannot be denied, however, that he does his best to narrow the gulf between the natural and the supernatural.

This is most clearly seen in his views on contemplation, when he stresses its affective and non-discursive character. To explain this partial suspension of the soul's activities in contemplation, he analyses the structure of the soul itself, distinguishing in it several regions, according to the faculties brought into play. There is first the lower or sensitive part, which uses and acts on the knowledge derived from the senses. Then comes the higher part, also called the intellectual or mental, which St Francis calls the spirit in the strict sense: here the soul uses the knowledge not founded on sense experience. This part is itself divided into three levels. On the

5—P.-R.S.

first two the spirit continues to operate in a normal, discursive manner; on the first level it operates on the human sciences, on the second on the truths of the faith. The third level constitutes what the saint calls the supreme point of the spirit: here the activity of the spirit ceases to be discursive and enters the world of contemplation, but this supreme point is brought into action only by the supernatural truths, and this is also the point where the theological virtues come into play. This complicated theory amounts to saying that while contemplation is a supernatural activity, nevertheless it has its roots in the natural structure of the soul. To all appearances, these views are related to those of the Rheno-Flemish mystics on the centre of the soul, but what with them was a metaphysical point of view St Francis has taken in a psychological sense.

The saint's regard for the human element is seen again in his rejection of the abstract school's theory of annihilation. Canfield's presentation of it frightened him and he disapproved of the mystical part of the *Rule of Perfection*. He too conceives the end of the spiritual life as union with the divine essence, and he would certainly not be hostile to the idea of "by-passing", but to him this union is one of person with person, and the symbol which governs his thought is that of the child in his mother's arms, while for Canfield it is that of fusion. To the end of his life St Francis continued to oppose the idea of the supereminent life and the depersonalization it involves. This, incidentally, is one of the limitations of his system. By toning down the extreme aspects of mysticism he denied himself the chance of thoroughly analysing certain elements of the problem: passivity, purifying trials, the theopathic state. This reservation need not prevent our admiring the extraordinary richness of the *Treatise on the Love of God*, from which spiritual persons have never ceased to seek nourishment.

This perhaps partly explains why the saint's early disciples, while remaining on the whole faithful to his teaching, unconsciously brought to it their own contributions. At the head of these early Salesians we must naturally place St Jane Frances de Chantal (1572–1641), a restless and tormented soul, who through agonizing interior trials experienced very high mystical states. She had no wish to be a spiritual author, but she became so through the posthumous publication of her letters in 1644. Unfortunately she had destroyed nearly all those she had sent to St Francis. In many respects, one must admit, her experiences surpassed those of her director. She was attracted to a very simple, non-conceptual form of contemplative prayer, which she describes under a definitely passive aspect and calls the prayer of "simple committal (*remise*) to God".[1] Often she seems to see it as the type of prayer which should be attained by her Visitation Sisters. On the other hand, her crucifying experiences of passive purifications enabled her to write some magnificent, poignant passages on this subject. In all this there is no question of disloyalty to her director. But there are very often subtle nuances, the tendency to abstractness, the emphasis on passivity, which give the impression that we are in another atmosphere, nearer to Canfield and his "supereminent life". Was there in this, perhaps, some shadow of misunderstanding, which might explain why in his later years Francis seems a little estranged from Mme de Chantal? Perhaps he felt himself rather superseded. In fact, if the Visitation Order has on the whole followed the impulse given it by its founder, its first generations were still imbued with the spirituality of St Jane Frances de Chantal.

In contrast, Jean-Pierre Camus, bishop of Belley (1584–1652), friend and disciple of St Francis de Sales, produced a literature quite disconcerting in its abundance, comprising more than a hundred and ninety titles. This flood has so far discouraged scholars, and we still await the monograph which

[1] This "prayer of simple committal" is the equivalent state to St John of the Cross' "prayer of loving attention". See Dom Cuthbert Butler, *Western Mysticism*, 2nd edition, containing "Afterthoughts", London, Constable, 1927, p. xix.

will revive his thought. Dispersed in innumerable works and sometimes distorted by polemics, this thought is not always very coherent. Camus claims that he too is a faithful disciple of St Francis, but his spiritual culture, which was very wide, has modified his Salesianism with many other influences, notably the Rhenish Flemings and the abstract school, along with the Italians and the Spaniards. Typical of his attitude is his *Direction for Mental Prayer* (1616), which appeared in St Francis' lifetime. He presents it as complementary to the *Introduction to the Devout Life* and mentions the same authors as those listed by the saint in his preface to the *Treatise on the Love of God*. He seems to have borrowed discreetly from Canfield, however, especially in the place he allots to the passive element in the spiritual life. But later, especially in his Mystical Theology (1640), he appreciably modified his views on this point; he went so far as to state clearly that every interior state is at once active and passive and that the two states are separated only by a difference of psychological perspective. He ranged himself against Canfield's idea of the "supereminent life", but in compensation for all this he introduced to his system the notions of "acquired" and "infused" contemplation, of which he seems certainly to have been one of the first theorists; we may note that Camus identifies this infused element with sanctifying grace. On the other hand, like St Francis, he only reluctantly makes room in his views for the higher states of unity. There can thus be no doubt that his attitude represents a certain recoil from the mysticism to which he bears witness. To complete his spiritual portrait we should recall that he impetuously crossed swords with the Jesuit Sirmond in defence of perfectly disinterested charity—"pure love".

CARDINAL DE BÉRULLE (1575–1629)

Parallel with the Salesian contribution, French spirituality was enriched by the work of Bérulle with new elements which, like the former, were continually developed throughout the century; but the founder of the Oratory, even more than the bishop of Geneva, was conscious of the originality of his contribution and did not hesitate to fight in defence of his ideas. This attachment was due perhaps to the fact that they were hardly won, at the price of an almost complete rupture with the circle of his formation. It was in fact in the circle of his cousin Mme Acarie and in the atmosphere of the abstract school that the young Pierre de Bérulle's piety first flowered, and we have noticed Dom Beaucousin's influence on him. In 1603–4 he was the heart and soul of the animated negotiations which led to the establishment of the Discalced Carmelites in France; he remained passionately attached to the Carmel, to which, in conjunction with Duval and Gallemant, he was appointed at first superior, and later (1614) visitor for life. He had also been searching, not without some hesitation, for the way of his own destiny. At one time he had thoughts of joining the Society of Jesus and in 1602, from August 28th to September 12th, he had actually made the *Exercises* with the Jesuits at Verdun. We still have the notes he made of this retreat; a simple adaptation, abstract in tendency, of Ignatian form: they show that Bérulle had not yet worked out his own spirituality. Only later, and partly, no doubt, under the influence of the picturesque Adrien Bourdoise, parish priest of St Nicolas du Chardonnet and founder of one of the first French seminaries, did he discover his vocation of working for the reform of the secular clergy. With this intention, in 1611, he founded the French Oratory. By that time he had already for some years been in possession of his essential ideas. Some historians tend to think that Bérulle's evolution developed continuously in a straight line from his *Brief Discourse on Interior Abnegation* and his retreat at Verdun. But this seems hardly tenable, and everything points to a decisive turning-point having taken place between 1605 and 1608. From this time it is certain that Bérulle centred his piety entirely on the mystery of the Incarnation, and that Jesus was for him not only the way but the goal of the spiritual life.

This excludes the "by-passing" theme, common to the northern mystics; on the theocentricism of the abstract school Bérulle superimposed Christocentricism.

What were the influences which helped Bérulle to form his personal synthesis? It is not easy to say. We can no longer believe, as was believed some forty years ago, that he was self-taught, constructing his whole system with no more equipment than the Bible, his Sorbonne lectures and some readings from the Fathers. His spiritual horizon was actually very rich and extensive, and all sorts of elements contributed to it. No doubt he was opposed to the Rhenish Flemings in rejecting the idea of by-passing, but they provided him not only with a very intense conviction of the divine primacy but with magnificent developments on the Incarnation and on union with Christ. One may ask through what channel these ideas reached him. Some have thought it was the *Pearl of the Gospel* which Bérulle certainly knew, but the resemblances are only superficial. In fact, as has lately been proved, we must go back to Harphius, to whom Bérulle owes much. All the evidence shows that among the Spaniards he was influenced by Juan de Avila and Luis de Leon; St Teresa perhaps helped to recall his attention to Christ. The Spanish Carmelites whom he had introduced to France to make foundations were in every way Teresan in spirit, and the most famous of them, Anne of Jesus, to whom St John of the Cross had dedicated his *Canticle,* always vowed she could understand nothing of the abstract spirituality taught to the first French novices. Now, among these Carmelites Bérulle was very intimate with Anne of St Bartholomew, St Teresa's travelling companion, and this friendship dates from the decisive years of his formation.

His debt to the Italians is a little harder to determine. He certainly borrowed some ideas from Pico della Mirandola's *Discourse on the Dignity of Man,* and he must have known the Italian spiritual authors when he wrote the *Brief Discourse;* like almost all of his period he was influenced to some extent by St Catherine of Genoa. Naturally, much must be credited to strictly theological sources, among which he seemed to prefer St Bonaventure to St Thomas. Above all, he must have made rich discoveries in the reading of the Fathers. During these years the demands of controversy with the Protestants obliged him to master Patristic theology at first hand, and his reading brought him into touch with a theology which was a living thing, blossoming into spirituality. He grasped it with both hands. He quotes Pseudo-Dionysius only rarely but he lives in his atmosphere and Dionysian themes abound in his works. Augustine is naturally the supreme Master, as he was to all that century, but Bérulle is relatively original in drawing inspiration from the Greek Fathers. In all this there is no question of servile imitation. Bérulle reconsiders all these borrowings in the light of his own system and it is precisely this elaboration which makes it so difficult to detect his sources. We may add that while the main lines of Bérulle's synthesis were soon laid down, the details on many points can only have been defined in the course of the years, and it seems that up to the publication of *The State and the Glories of Jesus*, in 1623, these variations were fairly important. Unfortunately there are so few dated documents that all reconstitution is uncertain, and in practice one is often compelled to be content with the final form of Bérulle's thought.

The synthetic aspect of this thought is very striking. To try to distinguish between its theology and its spirituality would be to falsify it in its essentials. On the other hand, it is important to analyse it in its whole extent. Urban VIII— when or where is not known—is said to have given Bérulle the title of Apostle of the Incarnate Word, and when the *Complete Works* were published in 1644 Fr Bourdoing's preface tried to present Bérulle's system solely in function of the Incarnation. This is to underrate the importance of the passages which speak of God in himself, and especially of the Trinity. On this point his contemplation derives from the Greek Fathers: he likes to see in the life of the Trinity a certain hierarchy in equality, and to insist on the proper rôle of each person. He sees in the Trinity a sort of pattern which is repeated from end to end of the divine work, as much in Creation as in the Incarnation and the Redemption. In his eyes the Son, the second person of the Trinity, is disposed to the Incarnation by his very rôle in the life of the Trinity. The Incarnation, of course, would not have taken place but for sin, which has made it in some way necessary, but in Jesus, the God-Man, the union of the Godhead and the Manhood presents a sort of fitness, which is as it were the basis of the Incarnation. Bérulle explains this fitness by dint of some rather laboured scholastic notions, but they serve to give his ideas a firm theological foundation. With the God-Man a new order, of which Christ is the principle, appears in the world, and Bérulle examines all its characteristics. The Incarnation, then, modifies in every way the problem of the relations between man and God. Henceforth it is unthinkable to look for the divinity apart from the Incarnation, that is, from the humanity of Christ, and this statement suffices to eliminate the idea of "by-passing". Jesus is the sole true and perfect adorer of the Father; every relation between man and God passes through him. Concerning sinful human nature Bérulle has a rather gloomy view, imbued with Augustinian pessimism. Only Christ's intervention can effect a remedy for this tragic wretchedness, and Christian spirituality can only be constructed in the framework of the Incarnation. It is in this perspective that we must examine Bérulle's views on the Christian's interior life.

Man, being created by God, is obliged to honour God, but the stain of original sin prevents him fulfilling this obligation. Only incorporation into Christ by baptism makes it possible for him to return to God. At that point he becomes bound to honour God not only by his nature but by his state as a Christian. Here the theme is obviously Pauline. Bérulle develops it in a very characteristic manner by analysing the Christian's interior attitude, by which this incorporation must be realized. He calls this "adherence". Adherence has its basis in baptismal grace and is therefore part of the very definition of a Christian. But Bérulle is original in requiring the Christian to make a voluntary, conscious effort to conform all his interior life, in every moment of his life, to the interior life of Jesus, to what he calls the states of the Incarnate Word. It is not a matter of mere imitation which, however perfect it may be, leaves us external to Christ. This conformity must result in a genuine transfusion into us of the very being of Jesus, of his prayer, his feelings, his adoration. If Bérulle was here inspired by certain considerations of Ludolph the Carthusian, he went much further than medieval piety, which saw the life of Christ as a tapestry of examples; much further too than the *Pearl* or Harphius, for whom union with Christ was only a way of access to the Godhead. By adherence Jesus becomes our life and our all, the way but also the goal. But we must note that in Bérulle's view the soul, without by-passing Christ, attains divinity itself in him, and is united to it, and we could say that by adherence the soul participates, in a way, in the hypostatic union.

On the other side, this adherence supposes perfect detachment from all that is not God: the soul must be separated not only from the whole created world but even from those gifts of God to which it might be attached, from even the highest supernatural favours. In some respects Bérulle here agrees with certain aspects of Canfield's views on "annihilation", and in fact uses this term fairly often. For the interior life of Jesus to pass into us there must be on our part the possibility of reception, which Bérulle calls "capacity". One must then strive to create this possibility in oneself, to become pure capacity for Christ and his life, and this corresponds to a negative effort which Bérulle calls abnegation or annihilation. Like Canfield, he sees this annihilation under an active and also a passive aspect, in which the divine power intervenes, to conduct the soul through the paths of suffering. The first objective of this annihilation is obviously sin and its consequences in us; but the mark of sin is so deep in man that for this annihilation to be effective it must extend to certain elements of nature itself. Bérulle refuses to abolish nature, since it is the work of God, but it was through the use of nature that sin invaded mankind. Man must therefore restrain this use by constant mortification, or rather he must submit it entirely to God's good pleasure. Here, too, Bérulle adopts some of Canfield's voluntarism, but apparently without going as far as the depersonalization which for Canfield marks the supereminent life.

Adherence too has its active and passive aspects. For while the Christian has to strive with his whole soul to enter into the interior life of Christ, in the last analysis it is Christ himself who comes to him by grace. Jesus acts in the soul by his spirit, which is the Holy Spirit: adherence is the work of the Spirit in us. Here Bérulle adopts some ideas dear to the Greek Fathers, but he does not make use of the magnificent insights of the Rhenish Flemings on the rôle of the gifts of the Holy Spirit in the mystical life: perhaps he thought they had too psychological a flavour. Like most authors of the seventeenth century he insists strongly on inner loyalty to the inspirations of the Holy Spirit, but with such discretion that he quite naturally avoids illuminism. He sees in every soul something unique and irreplaceable, which neither objective standards nor reasoning suffice to discover: its own way, that is; God's design for it, the particular manner in which God intends it to realize adherence. What this way is, only the Holy Spirit can make known to the soul. The soul must then be attentive to his motions and abandon itself wholly to God without wanting to choose for itself: this attitude too forms part of its annihilation.

Adherence therefore constitutes a fact of the spiritual life, far above its conscious realizations. The Christian must adhere to the interior states of the Incarnate Word, just as much in simple discursive meditation as in the highest paths of ecstasy. Sometimes Bérulle even seems to confuse contemplation with adherence. These views allow him, if we may put it so, to pay due honour to conceptual and discursive prayer. For him it is no longer an elementary degree reserved for beginners. Adherence fills all his life with a theology both profound and subtle, and causes it to penetrate to the unsearchable riches of Christ himself. In prayer there is no question of a method, with complicated articulations designed to mask the intellectual poverty of the process; it is a docile abandonment to the illuminations and prayer of the Holy Spirit in us, where prayer and religious inquiry combine in a harmonious synthesis. Such is the principle of Bérulle's "elevation", examples of which abound in his works, where lyricism and dialectic depth unite. Contrary to what has sometimes been claimed, this position in no way made Bérulle hostile or even indifferent to the mystical forms of spirituality. He knew many examples of them in his own circle and among those he directed, and on several occasions he was known to take private revelations very seriously. As occasion offered, he was even careful to integrate certain aspects of the problem into his system, especially that of passive purifications, which he holds to be the ways of suffering willed by God as a specially intimate adherence to the passion of Christ. Still, it is certain that he was never concerned to construct a coherent theory of the mystical states as such: the centre of his interest is elsewhere.

We can now appreciate better the novelty of Bérulle's synthesis, which in many respects was a reaction against both humanism and the abstract school. As might be expected, this aroused opposition. A great part of Bérulle's life was taken up with polemics, in which spirituality was mixed with politics and personal enmities. The foundation of the Oratory embroiled him with the Society of Jesus, which carried on its work in much the same field. Political differences set him against Richelieu. But it was over the Carmelite Order that the most violent struggles took place. Bérulle tried to win over all the French Carmels to his Christological spirituality, and very early, probably about 1612, he began for this purpose to use a formula of oblation which he had composed, entitled *A Vow of Servitude to Jesus and Mary*. The abstract school had many supporters among the nuns and even among the directors, and he encountered spirited resistance. In 1615, at a canonical visitation of the Carmel at Châlon, he wanted to impose his vow of servitude on all the nuns, and a real storm broke out.

The opposition was led by the two other superiors of the Carmelites, Duval and Gallemant, and also to some extent by Mme Acarie, now a Carmelite. A little before her death, in February 1618, Bérulle had a painful discussion with her at the Pontoise Carmel, in which he displayed great passion. Duval having succeeded in obtaining an unfavourable opinion on the vow from Cardinal Bellarmine, all stood firm on their positions. Besides this Bérulle was on very bad terms with the Discalced Carmelite friars, who had been introduced to France soon after the nuns, and thought they had a right to their government. Up to now the text of the vow of servitude had been kept more or less secret. But in 1620 the Carmelite friars succeeded in discovering a copy in the cell of a nun of Bordeaux who had just died. They immediately obtained censures against the vow from the Flemish theological faculties, including the famous Jesuit theologian Lessius. In France these censures provoked a regular war of pamphlets, in which Bérulle obtained equally brilliant approbations on his side. He succeeded, however, in dominating the debate, and in order to sum up the defence of his ideas in a monumental and decisive treatise he published in 1623 his twelve *Discourses on the State and the Glories of Jesus*, a magnificent synthesis, which puts him in the front rank of French spiritual authors. But it must be admitted that the memory of Bérulle will always be rather overshadowed by these conflicts which darkened his life.

THE SOCIETY OF JESUS

Settled in France in 1556, the Jesuits there spread rapidly, despite the opposition of the Gallicans, Parliament and the University, and in 1610 they already had about forty-five houses with more than fourteen hundred members. They were found in all classes of society, but naturally they penetrated the aristocracy most intensely, since many of the young nobles were educated in their colleges. The spiritual complexion of the French Jesuits was more complicated than is sometimes thought, and there is too strong a tendency to view it only from the angle of devout humanism. By this we mean an attempt at compromise between humanism and Christian piety, something sensibly different from Erasmism, though preserving some of its features. The devout humanists, even more than Erasmus, took an optimistic view of human nature. Like Pico della Mirandola, they held that man is the supreme masterpiece of God's handiwork, and that man glorifies God by developing all his potentialities harmoniously through the free exercise of his faculties. Without eliminating the notion of sin they did their best to minimize its importance and to set store upon all that man can achieve by his unaided natural powers. On this ground they did not hesitate to cite examples from the virtues of the pagans. They tried to omit the painful aspects of asceticism and to empty mortification of almost all its reality. Christianity thus becomes a philosophical ideal which to some extent ensures us happiness in this life, or at least enables us to bear calmly the inevitable blows of fate. Christian morality is reduced to a sort of mean between theocentric and anthropocentric systems, each of which has a right to a certain place in the scheme. Man thus recovers his place in the sight of God and also his place in the world. Devout humanism, in fact, extends its optimism to the whole world: it sees it purely as a work of God designed to lead souls to himself. The use of creatures must therefore be governed by a wise temperance, but the idea of a self-denial whose only motive is penitence is foreign to it, and always the soul must seek God first through the beauties of the world. Where Erasmus would recall the themes of Flemish piety which nurtured his youth, or guide the soul to a purified and fully interior piety, the devout humanists were satisfied with a very superficial cosmism. Nor do we find in them much of that profound feeling for the Bible which makes Erasmus' work so attractive, in spite of its faults.

These are of course only schematic and general features, within which the devout humanists displayed their countless personal variations. An attempt was made, some decades ago, to revive them, but it must be confessed that they expressed themselves in works which are usually unreadable and cumbered with a formidable load of mythology. Besides, the group would have to be more accurately defined than hitherto. To be a devout humanist it is not enough to have a certain optimism and to borrow metaphors from antiquity or the gods of Olympus: neither St Francis de Sales nor Camus belong to the group. Moreover, devout humanism was in no way the speciality of the Society of Jesus. Authors of this school were found among seculars as among most of the religious orders. It is generally agreed that the quintessence of devout humanism is found in the works of a magistrate, Guillaume du Vair (1556–1621), whose *Holy Philosophy* appeared in 1588, and still more in those of a canon, Pierre Charron (1541–1603), whose treatise *On Wisdom* (1601) continued to be republished and read during the first three quarters of the seventeenth century. This book sets us some singular problems, by the way, for though the free-thinkers contributed to its success a pious Berullian like Saint-Cyran vigorously defended it, which shows that Charron's thought was open to different interpretations. On the other hand it was a Capuchin, Yves de Paris (1590–1678), who prolonged the tendencies of devout humanism far into the century.

It is certain, nevertheless, that many Jesuits were obliged by the demands of their mission to adopt positions of this sort. It was in fact by as advanced an assimilation as possible that they penetrated society in their time: they would not be ignorant of any of the problems and currents of thought affecting their contemporaries. On the contrary, they identified themselves with them as far as loyalty to their vocation permitted. Many of them, through the very high level of their literary education, had access to a humanism which naturally became a devout humanism. This is often regarded as a consequence of Molinism, but that is to reverse the relationship. Molina's *Concordia* appeared in 1588, and by that time, in Flanders and France, if not in Spain, humanist tendencies were firmly established in Jesuit circles. It is only fair to say that Molina's theological theses, and those of Lessius, fitted wonderfully into the movement and gave it some doctrinal basis. But among the many French Jesuits of this period who have left us spiritual works it would be vain to search for the ideal representative of devout humanism: in actual fact each took part in his own way and according to his own position. The whole subject requires thorough research.

Because of the great extent of his work, the name of Louis Richeome (1544–1625) is one of the first to spring to mind. True, a great part of his work is devoted to anti-Huguenot polemic. His books of piety present a picture of man which is optimistic to the point of *naïveté*: a good example is his *Farewell of the Devout Soul on leaving the Body* (1601, perhaps 1590), in which original sin is a mere scar and the desire of human glory is practically a virtue. As for the famous Fr François de Garasse (1585–1631), who specialized in polemics against the free-thinkers (sometimes with more zeal than discretion), he carries concessions to naturalism to an extreme. At times he seems in a curious way to set God and man on a sort of equality, like two merchants doing business: when man has paid God his due, he is clear. Thus human life, in his view, has a twofold end, one part is for God, the other for man. He too is disconcertingly optimistic and claims to find the equivalent of the evangelical virtues in the pagans.

In this he prepares the way for Fr Antoine Sirmond (1590–1643) who, in his *Defence of Virtue* (1641), maintains that the good deeds of the pagans have merit for heaven. The same Sirmond gives a strangely evanescent interpretation of the commandment of charity when he says that we are commanded not so much to love God as not to hate him; that the mere observance of the moral law suffices to keep the commandment, and that we cannot define any point in our lives when we are obliged to make an act of love to God. These opinions incurred the attacks of Camus and later furnished weapons to the great Arnauld and to Pascal.

In point of fact Sirmond and Garasse are extreme cases and on the whole their brethren in religion held more moderate positions. This is true of Fr Etienne Binet (1569–1639). There can be no doubt how highly he was esteemed by the devout, and he was on good terms with St Francis de Sales, St Jane Frances and Mother Angélique Arnauld. There are some fine passages in his work. In 1623 he published his *Solid Practice of the Holy Love of God*. Contrary to what has sometimes been held, Binet's ideas have no connection with Berullism, but the "pacts of love" which he advised sprang from a very intense feeling of charity and led him to write some very evocative passages on the Heart of Jesus. We find the same atmosphere in the work which is probably his masterpiece: *Of the All-Powerful Attraction of the Love of Jesus Christ, and the Earthly Paradise* (1631), some chapters of which bear comparison with St Francis de Sales, while others, it must be confessed, betray a lamentable lack of taste. But in other respects one cannot doubt that Binet belongs to devout humanism. His *Consolation and Encouragement for the Sick* (1616) has perhaps been too harshly criticized, but there are indeed some traces of Pelagianism in the way he represents devotion as something easy and almost natural. In his controversy with Saint-Cyran over the *Private Chaplet of the Blessed Sacrament* (1633) he showed that he understood nothing about mysticism or even the contemplative aspect of religion. Elsewhere he advises the Christian to fling himself heart and soul into the world's affairs and to prove himself keener and more active in them than others. For the rest, the idea common to Garasse and Binet, that the Christian life is easy, decided his path. It is found again in a little book to which the *Provincial Letters* gave unintentional publicity, the *Easy Devotion* (1652) of Fr Pierre Lemoyne (1602–71); the charm of its style should not blind us to the fact that it reduces the most traditional demands of Christianity to vanishing point.

There are other names which lead us to a more interior piety. Here we must again recall the attractive personality of Fr Pierre Coton (1564–1626), the indulgent confessor of Henry IV, rivalling St Francis de Sales in his zeal to acclimatize a genuine and not merely easy devotion among men of the world. With him may be associated Fr Nicolas Caussin (1583–1651), Louis XIII's confessor: he too, in his *Holy Court* (1624), brought within reach of the world an uncompromising piety. It is known too that Fr Caussin centred his piety on a very intense notion of charity which undoubtedly tended to "pure love"—and if he did defend Fr Sirmond, that was probably more out of loyalty to his Order than from personal conviction. Still in the same line, we meet another royal confessor in Fr Jean Suffren (1571–1641). His *Christian Year* is a magnificent book which deserves to be better known. The rule of life put before the faithful is austere and exacting, but bathed in prayer and the sense of the presence of God. While the way he offers the soul is at first that of ordinary prayer or meditation, he gives it glimpses of mystical or extraordinary prayer which are evidently inspired by Luis de la Puente. Finally, it is very surprising that total oblivion should have overtaken a masterpiece like the *Spiritual Institution* (1643) of Fr Nicolas du Sault, steeped as it is in the mysticism of Luis de la Puente, and full of quotations from Blosius, St Teresa and Gerson. It contains some pages on pure love which leave Camus far behind and would have enraptured Fénelon.

The case of Fr du Sault brings us at last to the problem
so often raised: the existence of a mystical current among the
French Jesuits. The question is specially acute concerning the
famous Fr Louis Lallemant (1587–1635), on whom we still
await a really satisfactory study, but it is very hard to find a
clear solution. Fr Lallemant exerted his influence mainly
through his words and example, and it was certainly very
strong from 1628 to 1630, the period when he was performing
the duties of instructor to the tertians at Rouen: that is, he
was responsible for the religious who, after some ten years of
formation, spent a third year of novitiate before making their
solemn vows. On this picked audience Fr Lallemant had a
profound effect. But he was never a spiritual author: he published nothing and we have nothing from his pen but a few
short letters. His *Spiritual Doctrine* was published by Fr
Champion only in 1694, from notes taken at the tertianship
conferences by Fr Rigoleuc and Fr Surin, and it is very hard
to tell how much of it is derived from these. Besides this, some
little treatises drawn up by Fr Rigoleuc must also be due to
Fr Lallemant's addresses. It must then be granted that Fr
Lallemant's thought is known to us only indirectly and
probably very incompletely, and that any attempt to restate
it must be largely guesswork. Moreover, our documents give
us the state of this thought round about 1630, but tell us
nothing about its sources.

By this time Fr Lallemant's views were fully formed, and
this simple fact is enough to decide the question of his
Berullism, which has raised such passionate and embittered
discussion these last thirty years. At Bérulle's death in 1629
his works had still a very small circulation and the *Glories
of Jesus* was considered primarily a work of controversy. In
this quarrel the main body of the Jesuits had sided against
the Cardinal, and it is unlikely that Lallemant would have
sought the elements of his formation from the founder of the
Oratory. One of his letters proves, however, that he knew and
liked some of Bérulle's minor works: he probably meant the

little manuscript essays which circulated in the Carmels, many of which are found in the *Works of Piety*, but this liking arises from Lallemant's finding something of his own ideas in Bérulle's works, not from any idea of being his disciple. Everything suggests that Lallemant owed his spirituality to his own formation, which took place long before the *Glories*. He himself kept his tertian year at Paris in 1615–16, and if we knew more about the background of the Paris Jesuits at that period, one of the keys to the problem would be in our hands. At that very time, as we have seen, they produced a translator for Harphius, which allows us to believe that the Flemish mystics, perhaps even the abstract school, met with sympathy among them. It is possible that Lallemant there encountered complex influences, among which mysticism held an important place.

The problem of the sources of the *Spiritual Doctrine* has never been seriously studied and the controversies already mentioned have not contributed much to it. Here we can only tell what is revealed by a rapid examination. Fr Lallemant remains in general faithful to the Ignatian tradition, but he inflects it in a mystical sense, such as we have found among the Jesuits of Spain. Now it is these Spanish precedents which are very important in his case, for he owes much to Luis de la Puente, and particularly to his biography of Balthazar d'Alvarez. Besides him, he had certainly read Luis de Granada, Juan de Avila and St Teresa, and borrowed some ideas from them. On the other side he was familiar with the Rheno-Flemish school and moved in their ambit. He was perhaps inspired by the *Pearl*, but his real master was clearly Harphius. Some allusions here and there remind one of Canfield.

The real working of his thought escapes us: the rather artificial plan of the *Doctrine* is the work of Fr Champion, who has regrouped the notes he had in his hands with moderate success. But this grouping clearly illustrates certain fundamental themes of his spirituality. There is first his theocentricism, by which he is definitely opposed to humanist tendencies and says that man's sole greatness lies in subjection to God. Man must therefore seek nothing but God alone and his glory, by-passing all creatures, not even resting in God's gifts, which are yet not God. To arrive at this, two things are necessary: purification of the heart and absolute docility to the Holy Spirit. By purity of heart Lallemant means first the rejection of the slightest inclination towards sin, but it goes further: the soul must break with its affective attachments, even those that are innocent. His thought, at least according to the *Doctrine*, stops at this point and he does not go on to the idea of the nakedness of the spirit, dear to the abstract school. On abandonment to the inner guidance of the Holy Spirit, he draws on the ideas already current among French spiritual authors. Unlike Bérulle, he uses the convenient scheme based on the seven gifts of the Spirit, but his views on this point are elementary in comparison with the vast mystical horizons here introduced by the Flemish mystics, to whom the succession of the gifts corresponds to the stages of the interior path. Lallemant is faithful to Ignatian directives in recommending the use of reflection on oneself, introspection and the discernment of spirits. He dilates at length, too, on union with Jesus, the Incarnate Word. On this subject the *Doctrine* has some very fine passages, in which he shows that the idea of a God-Man is a sort of limiting of the divine power. It is here that the problem of his relation with Bérulle is most important. But it must not be forgotten that these passages were composed at a later date, when certain Berullian expressions had become current coin in France. Actually, none of Bérulle's really original great themes appear in them. On the other hand, in spite of a difference of style, it is easy to recognize a surprising similarity with corresponding passages in Harphius.

Finally, Fr Lallemant's counsels on prayer undoubtedly tend to lead his disciples towards contemplation, and here he seems to link up with Balthazar d'Alvarez, as far as he knew him through Luis de la Puente. On some points he is equally inspired by St Teresa. The last pages of the *Doctrine*, unfortunately all too short, bring us to the heart of the mystical problem and broach the Dionysian theme of the divine darkness, in an atmosphere which is that of the abstract school. Though Fr Lallemant cites a vision of St Ignatius as one of his examples, such advanced mysticism understandably aroused some alarm. In the end the General, Mutius Vitelleschi, censured Fr Lallemant's spirituality as contrary to the spirit of the Society. His teaching at Rouen was stopped, but this censure did not check the spread of his ideas.

CHAPTER IV

THE ZENITH OF FRENCH SPIRITUALITY

The term "French school" was introduced to spiritual literature some forty years ago and has been very popular, but its
use may be misleading if it gives the impression that at a
certain period French spiritual authors were practically unanimous. The truth is of course more complex. Among contemporary writers there always tends to be a certain community
of style and atmosphere. In the case of Christian spirituality
there is besides a whole vocabulary and fund of ideas which
are necessarily identical. But these obvious affinities should
not blind us to the differences which are also found, charac-
terizing groups and individuals. We have seen that the
spiritual revival which marked the early seventeenth century
in France was expressed in a common dynamism, within
which very distinct currents came to the surface. As we might
expect, these currents flowed on their subsequent ways, but
their development was not linear: there were ramifications
and cross-currents, producing intermediate types often difficult
to classify. Then again, in this period spiritual writing was
startlingly prolific: a complete inventory of it has yet to be
made. All one can do, then, is to point out certain specially
significant works which serve as landmarks in this mass of
literature and indicate its main orientations—always remem-
bering that it would be absurd to divide such categories into
water-tight compartments.

BERULLISM

Bérulle's work has both greatness and weakness, and perhaps the greatness is easier for us to appreciate than it was for his contemporaries, who were more shocked by certain deficiencies. His memory was overshadowed by polemics, and moreover his complete works could not be published till 1644, after the death of his enemy Richelieu. They had no great success, and his official biography, produced in 1646 by Germain Habert, abbot of Cérisy, remained in the bookshops. Already it was felt that Bérulle's work was outmoded, in some way superseded. Its prodigious wealth, by its very luxuriance, embarrassed a public which now demanded more order and clarity. Bérulle had employed the vocabulary and even the notions of scholasticism, just when scholasticism was being steadily discredited. Berullism needed to be simplified, pruned down and presented in the style of the day, and even his most loyal followers realized this and set themselves to do it, convinced that this was the best service they could render to a venerated memory.

One of the most interesting of these earliest disciples is the Oratorian Guillaume Gibieuf (1591–1650). Having joined the Oratory in 1612 as a convinced Molinist, he was not long in becoming an Augustinian under the influence of Bérulle, who gently reproached him for giving too little place to Christ in his ideas on grace. An excellent theologian, Gibieuf became also the defender of Berullism in the sphere of intellectual speculation, and Bérulle, at the end of his life, induced him to write a Latin treatise *On the Freedom of God and his Creatures*, which appeared in 1630. Hostile to Aristotelianism, which was then prevalent in the theological faculties, Gibieuf here showed himself to be steeped in Platonism. It is in the divine freedom itself that he sees the *idea* (in the Platonic sense) of human freedom, an idea whose perfect realization is found in Christ.

A similar metaphysical theory is found in his most famous

and probably best book, *The Life and Glories of the most holy Virgin Mary, Mother of God* (1637), in which he fully exploits the great themes of Berullian theology. Bérulle had already written much on our Lady, but Gibieuf summed it all up in a synthetic exposition, obviously inspired by the *Glories of Jesus*. He is, besides, so conscious of being Bérulle's successor that he does not hesitate to borrow at times from some of the unpublished texts he had in his hands, for at the same time he was preparing the publication of the Cardinal's complete works. He contemplates the Blessed Virgin solely in the context of the Incarnation and admits us to the council of the divine Persons as they predestinate her to giving a human nature to the Word. Gibieuf's Platonism here goes further than Bérulle's, and he is bold to say that the idea of the divine motherhood is pre-existent to the Blessed Virgin herself; it is in this sense that he interprets the scriptural texts on the uncreated Wisdom which Catholic liturgy traditionally applies to our Lady. Bérulle's exemplarism supplies him also with some fine flights of illustration: in the manner of his master he considers the Incarnation as a second Trinity, uniting the Father, Jesus and Mary; in the same line of thought he builds up a whole system of parallels between the rôle of the Father and that of our Lady. Repeating a favourite expression of Bérulle's, he recalls that the Blessed Virgin is at the source of a deified humanity.

In Mary he sees the very type of Bérulle's adherence; he shows her throughout her life, partaking in all the states of the God-Man in perfect conformity, her soul corresponding to the dispositions of that of her divine Son, and to the eternal Father's counsels concerning him. He goes into detail and examines the movements of Mary's soul, her interior, as it was then called, in its different states. The whole constitutes a life of the Blessed Virgin, more or less analogous to that life of Jesus which Bérulle had undertaken, but which stops unfinished even before the Nativity. This is no mere treatise on Marian theology. Not only is the style that affective style commended by St Francis de Sales, but these marvellous "elevations" are filled with spiritual considerations. It is in perfect conformity with the spirit of his whole book that Gibieuf ends with a fervent exhortation to devotion towards Mary, our model, our principle and (after God and Jesus Christ) our end. Faithful to Bérulle's vocabulary and to the ideas of his own treatise *On Freedom*, he reminds us that the servitude on which we enter in respect of God's sovereignty is our real freedom. This fine book, now, alas, unprocurable, makes us regret that Fr Gibieuf produced so little in the way of spiritual literature.

Fr François Bourgoing (1585–1662), who in 1641 became the third superior-general of the Oratory, was another who proved himself a faithful interpreter of Berullism and made himself its popularizer, if we may so describe him. His activity in the administration of the Oratory began in the critical period after Bérulle's death: it needs to be more closely studied, but it is no exaggeration to say that he saved the founder's work. It was he who published Bérulle's complete works, prepared by Gibieuf, and provided them with a long preface. These pages are an excellent résumé of Berullian spirituality, which has remained a classic to the present day, though it perhaps rather underrates the importance of the Trinitarian theme.

Bourgoing seems early to have realized that there was something abrupt and inaccessible in Bérulle's work, and so he undertook to make it current on the level of popular piety. He did this on the Cardinal's death with the publication of his *Truths and Excellencies of our Lord Jesus Christ*, which appeared in Latin in 1629 and in a French translation, considerably developed, in 1636. These meditations, in which Berullism is expounded on a methodical plan and in a clear form, had considerable success: it seems that they went through some thirty editions during the century and that Richelieu himself held them in great esteem. At the head of his work Bourgoing placed a *Direction for Mental Prayer* which was his own contribution, since Bérulle had composed no rules on this subject. Here he proves himself flexible and discreet; reminding us that prayer is not a work of man but a gift of grace and an infusion of the Holy Ghost, he advises us to make a reasonable use of methods and invites the soul to an interior tension which should normally lead it out of discursive ways of prayer. The meditations prescribed by Bourgoing are good examples of Bérulle's "elevations", somewhat too sober in style, perhaps, but with the difficult points of the system clearly explained.

Like Gibieuf he draws on the vocabulary of Platonism, and considers our Lord the worthiest, the most divine, the most excellent *idea* ever conceived in the divine intelligence. Christ is the archetype of the Christian, and his predestination is the exemplar, the source and the cause of ours. At a time when men had just lately witnessed the triumphant ascendancy of Aristotelianism it is significant to note that Bérulle's first disciples resorted to Platonism to expound their master's ideas. With Bourgoing this tendency may possibly be an expression of his sympathy with the Flemish mystics. On the problem of the Incarnation, he admits with Bérulle that it took place only on account of sin. But in the manner of Harphius he likes to insist also on the fact that the purpose of the Incarnation was to uplift, sanctify and deify human nature, as well as to give God the only true adoration which could render him man's debt. But on the whole it is the great Berullian themes which haunt Bourgoing's work, all methodically set forth for practical adaptation to concrete situations: it was in this spirit that he composed several *Retreat Exercises*. Naturally, all this rather clips the wings of Berullian lyricism, but it preserved its influence for a long time.

In the same spiritual succession comes the name of Jean Duvergier de Hauranne, abbot of Saint-Cyran (1581–1643). For a long time his true character has been distorted in very different senses by the Jansenist controversies, but recent studies have made clear that he should be regarded as one of the most striking figures of the Counter-Reformation and one of Berullism's great champions. He had begun his career with a worldly period, morally blameless but haunted by vast ambitions, and his first works, the *Royal Question* (1609) and the *Apologia for La Rocheposay* (1615), make a display of casuistic virtuosity which reveal him as a former pupil of the Jesuits. About 1618, on his ordination as priest, his interior life began to evolve: he renounced his too human aspirations and turned to a more austere and demanding Christianity. His spirituality, however, was still somewhat undecided until the day in 1620 when the foundation of a college of the Oratory in Poitiers, where he lived, put him in touch with Condren, and then with Bérulle. Between Saint-Cyran and Bérulle an intimate friendship sprang up, which was renewed when a little later the two friends rediscovered each other in Paris and had conversations five or six hours long. It was then Bérulle's greatest productive period, when he was writing the *Glories of Jesus*, and it is quite possible that Saint-Cyran collaborated in it to some extent. It is indeed very likely that Bérulle drew on the latter's prodigious patristic erudition, acquired chiefly during his long retreat at Camp-de-Prats from 1611 to 1614, in company with his friend Jansenius. Saint-Cyran's spiritual life thus developed in a wholly Berullian atmosphere.

Saint-Cyran lost no time in championing Bérulle's ideas, and he supported his complaints against the Jesuits. It was certainly in order to injure the prestige of the Society that in 1626 he directed against one of its principal members his *List of the Faults of Fr Garasse*. In the matter of the *Vow of Servitude* he was a keen supporter of Bérulle and fought fiercely on his side. When the Cardinal died in disgrace in 1629, Saint-Cyran gave public expression to his veneration for the dead man in an open letter to Fr Bourgoing, and from that day Richelieu turned against Saint-Cyran the hate he had formerly reserved for Bérulle. Naturally, Duvergier's spiritual writings bear traces of his Berullism. A few small treatises, unfortunately never published, show him to be faithful to his master, to the point of an almost servile reproduction of his ideas and vocabulary. But he had the wisdom to understand at once that for the Berullian theses to be effectively defended they must be freed from the thick outer shell which too often enveloped them. In conformity with the tendencies of his time towards the archaic, he tried to translate them into strictly patristic language. He was even more careful than Bérulle to get beyond theoretical viewpoints and stand on the ground of Christian piety and direction. It is chiefly in this field that Saint-Cyran's psychological interests led him into positions which were very individual, but were doubtless known and approved by Bérulle.

It was in 1627, in his work *On the New Heart*, that Saint-Cyran formulated, for the use of his disciple Chavigny, his theory of renewal. He is anxious to consider the Christian life from the point of view of stable states, not as a succession of transitory acts. The conversion which turns a sinner into a Christian, as well as that which leads the soul from an ordinary life to fervour, must be the response to a psychological shock which achieves a break with the past. Saint-Cyran's procedure for this purpose consists in putting the one under direction in the temporary state of a penitent, when he voluntarily forgoes Communion, and the confessor defers absolution. During this period of waiting the penitent must live in retreat, mortification and prayer. At the end of this delay, which Saint-Cyran thinks should be for several weeks, he is "reconciled" by confession and Communion. He must then live an austere and retired life, which will preserve the graces he has received. Saint-Cyran believed too that an ordinary layman could well live in retreat under the guidance of a director, without joining a religious order; this was a novelty for his time.

From 1633 Saint-Cyran's relations with Port-Royal gave him many opportunities of applying his theories, but their spread caused a stir among the public which reached its climax in the conversion of Mother Angélique's nephew, the brilliant advocate Antoine Lemaître, who became the first of the Solitaries of Port-Royal. Richelieu made this the pretext for imprisoning Saint-Cyran in the fortress of Vincennes; a totally arbitrary act, for it was followed by no trial. From his prison cell Saint-Cyran continued to extend his influence over a considerable number of people. His *Letters Christian and Spiritual*, published with considerable revision in 1645 and 1647, prove his devotion to Berullism, as do his private notes from which in 1670, at the cost of great editorial labour, were drawn his *Considerations on the Sundays and Feasts*. As for his penitential theories, he tended more and more to defend them on the ground that they were a return to the practice of the primitive Church. It was in this spirit that he induced his disciple Antoine Arnauld to write *Frequent Communion* in 1643.

Some of Bérulle's other successors were less faithful, in the sense that they did not shrink from constructing a synthesis out of Berullism and views derived from elsewhere. This was so, for example, with Fr Charles de Condren (1588–1641), Bérulle's successor as General of the Oratory. In some respects he was a puzzling personality, whose character it is not easy to discern exactly. It seems that from his childhood his natural tendencies were accentuated by curious mystical experiences which inclined him to a spirituality of annihilation. Through his studies at the Sorbonne he came in touch with André Duval, and everything suggests that he was then introduced to the ideas of the abstract school. Having joined the Oratory, he was exposed to Berullian influences without in any way giving up his own tendencies, and from Bérulle's Platonism he drew a mysticism of annihilation which is all his own. He likes to dwell on the incompatibility which separates the divine essence from the creature—a sheer nothing, which can do homage to God only by its very annihilation. The idea of sacrifice is central to Condren, but he sees it primarily as destruction, the homage of the nothing to the absolute Being. The sacrifice of sinful man cannot be accepted by God, and so follows a sort of necessity for the Incarnation, for only the God-Man can offer the divinity a worthy sacrifice. The Word clothes himself in human nature in order to have something to annihilate, and the prime object of the Incarnation is to provide matter for the perfect sacrifice, which is Christ's. Even so, this does not prevent the Incarnation being a sort of paradox: by uniting a creature to the divine essence it effects a contradiction in terms, implying, dare we say, a sort of state of violence.

Like Bérulle, Condren sets himself to study the different states of the Incarnate Word, but naturally his attention is specially directed to the state of victim. For him too, the Christian's fundamental attitude is summed up in the idea of adherence to Jesus. The first effect of this adherence is to make us enter on this victim-state of Christ, and this adherence itself brings about our sacrifice, for it is operated in us by the Holy Spirit, the Spirit of Jesus who comes into us to take possession of our whole being. Now there is such incompatibility between this divine Spirit and our sinful nature that in taking possession of man he destroys it in him, so to speak. These being the conditions of his thought, we can well understand that Condren insisted strongly on the theme of docility to the Holy Spirit, the inner guide, and that in his direction he laid much stress on the notion of indifference, of total abandonment to God. This is an interpretation of Berullism in terms of certain ideas of the abstract school, one which was to have great success. Perhaps through humility, or more likely from fear of responsibility, Condren published nothing in his lifetime, but in 1642 his *Letters and Discourses* were published and later often reprinted. In 1677 Fr Quesnel brought out his *Idea of Priesthood and the Sacrifice of Christ*, in which, albeit much retouched, some of Fr Condren's writings on sacrifice may be found.

One whole department of Condren's thought seems to have been preserved for us by a tiny work whose author is the

Oratorian Claude Séguenot (1596–1676): *The Conduct of Mental Prayer for Souls who have no Facility in it.* There is an apparently well-founded tradition to the effect that this work was written in collaboration with Fr de Condren, and in any case it is certain that Séguenot was profoundly influenced by him. Séguenot first lays down the principle that prayer is not the fruit of human effort but a gift of God, a grace; he therefore revolts against the rules and methods which ignore this fundamental truth and give too much place to effort. His opposition to methods is matched by an equally decided opposition to intellectualism. Prayer is not an operation of the mind. Reasoning, knowledge and even the highest lights go for little: nothing counts but union with God in charity. But God is so far exalted above the creature that the soul, for all its good will, cannot attain to him. He himself intervenes by giving us his Holy Spirit, who prays in us and unites us to himself. We must then abandon ourselves to the inner guidance of the Spirit and give up our own lights in order to enter into what Séguenot (with Pseudo-Dionysius) calls the divine darkness. So far from trying in prayer to lay hold of thoughts and reasonings, the soul should surrender completely to God's action in itself, should listen rather than speak, should live by faith. From this it has sometimes been argued that Séguenot was guilty of Quietism, but it is only fair to say that in his view passivity is never inactivity, and this abandonment to God involves very great effort and sometimes heroic fidelity. This fidelity is made possible for us by adherence to the states of Jesus, in such a way that our prayer is first the prayer of Jesus in us: here Séguenot joins hands with Bérulle, but on the whole his mysticism is that of Condren.

One of the most interesting of all Condren's disciples is Jean-Jacques Olier (1608–57), and it is a pity that no one has yet devoted to him the solid critical study which he deserves and needs: even his works are only partially published, and several in a most imperfect manner. Yet here we have one of the best representatives of the French school, and by his literary talent perhaps the most remarkable. M. Olier is known to have been converted after a considerable period of worldliness. Then, about 1635, he came under the direction of Condren, and for two years he experienced the most acute interior sufferings, perhaps connected with the hyper-sensitivity of an excessively nervous temperament, but there can be no doubt that they constituted his period of passive purification. For Olier was a mystic, a very great mystic who experienced the highest unitive states, and it was through his own interior atmosphere that he interpreted the themes of Bérulle and Condren. Like them he is steeped in Augustinian pessimism, but his long experience of dereliction enables him to speak of human misery with a truly poignant accent. The nothingness of the creature strikes him so forcibly that in his eyes the Incarnation must have taken place as it were by surprise, for if the humanity of Christ could have used its liberty it would have recoiled in holy fear from the divinity. When uniting himself with Christ in the Eucharist, Olier used to adore first the sovereignty of God, his right to annihilate the creature and destroy life. From such points of view, he rejoices to repeat the most vertiginous phrases in which Fr Condren's "naughting" is expressed. For him too, the first effect of adherence to the states of the incarnate Word is to annihilate the soul. But, no doubt more accurate in this than Condren, he deals first with the destruction of the old Adam, that is, with the creature as stained and soiled with sin. It is true that his pessimism makes him extend this staining very far: by the slightest return on himself, the slightest concession to self-love, man enters the kingdom of evil. In this, M. Olier prepares the way for those theories of the renunciation of self-love which flourished a little later, and shows himself in favour of a total, uncompromising resistance to all the desires of nature.

In some respects this rigorism can seem inhuman and terrifying. But in practice, as his letters of direction bear witness, M. Olier tempers it with much discretion and extremely penetrating understanding. Like his predecessors, he believes that in this sphere abandonment to the Holy Spirit is indispensable. Two traits, however, stamp him as really original. First, his mysticism, which in his published works is expressed with great caution, but holds a large place in his unpublished writings, and later exposed him to the scorn of Nicole and the anti-mystics. Then, the lyrical and poetical gifts with which he expresses his ideas, making him a writer of the first rank. Under this head, we cannot too greatly admire his *Christian Day* (1655), one of the very rare little books he published in his lifetime, in which, within the Berullian framework, he tries, like Fr Coton before him, to teach the Christian to sanctify all his actions. In another direction, it should be added that by founding the Society of St Sulpice he did more than anyone else to implant Bérulle's priestly spirituality among the clergy.

Among those of Bérulle's successors who were able to make a really personal synthesis out of the master's abundance, St John Eudes (1601–80) deserves a special place, for the importance and volume of his works. His spiritual formation was entirely Berullian, for he spent twenty years in the Oratory before leaving it in 1643 to found the Congregation of Jesus and Mary, which likewise spread Berullian piety in the seminaries. By this time he had already written one of his most important works: *The Life and Kingdom of Jesus in Christian Souls* (1637). This aims at presenting in clear and didactic form an idea of Christian life which is a practical application of Berullian adherence: that Jesus should be formed, sanctified, caused to live and reign in our souls. To Bérulle's influence he added Condren's: here and there St John Eudes uses ideas and perhaps passages which derive from Condren. As the years passed, his apostolic interests led him to express his Berullism in the form of a very concrete, practical piety, and of course to simplify some of its expressions, while still remaining very faithful to its general lines.

But then, just when he was about to resume his independence in order to carry out his great projects, he had a decisive encounter: during the summer of 1641, the incidence of his preaching work brought him to know Marie des Vallées (1590–1656), known as the Saint of Coutances. She was a pious girl of humble birth, who experienced mystical states of a high order, mixed with strange phenomena which her own circle attributed to diabolical possession, but would now probably be diagnosed as of neurotic origin. Otherwise, the case of Marie des Vallées in many respects resembles that of St Catherine of Genoa, by whose works she was certainly influenced.

St John Eudes always considered his meeting with Marie des Vallées to be one of the great graces of his life. He devoted three biographical essays to her, forming together a considerable volume, still not published, unfortunately. Later, in 1674, an enemy of his, Charles Dufour, abbot of Aunay, made this the ground of a formidable charge of Illuminism: the saint defended himself with spirit, but concealed nothing of his veneration for Marie des Vallées. How far was he influenced by her? It is hard to say, and there has been much exaggeration on the subject. But it must be granted that after 1641 his thought developed more and more on his own lines, and in particular he developed his views on devotion to the Hearts of Jesus and Mary and became the promoter of their liturgical cultus. Some modern commentators regard this as merely an outcome of his Berullism; others attach great importance to certain revelations of Marie des Vallées; it has also been suggested that his contacts with the Benedictines of Caen must have introduced him to the works of St Mechtilde and St Gertrude. But none of these theories seem sufficient, and even if they contain elements of truth they are not enough to explain the undoubted originality of the Eudist views, which must be credited to the author's own genius.

The symbolism of the heart was of course current in the seventeenth century, in connection with a voluntarist affec-

tivity, in which heart and will are identified. St John Eudes
accepts this meaning but exploits to the full all the wealth it
contains, symbolically associated with Christ's heart of flesh.
The Heart of Jesus thus becomes the object of a cult which
is essentially dogmatic, free from the "dolorist" sentimentality
sometimes urged against the devotion which sprang from
Paray-le-Monial. At first, in 1643, St John Eudes' Marian
piety led him to combine the Heart of Jesus and the Heart
of Mary in a united homage; then the desire for logical clear-
ness and theological accuracy led him to distinguish the two
Hearts, and it seems that at first he rather emphasized the
Heart of Mary. About 1669 he composed a liturgical office
of the Heart of Jesus, the feast of which was celebrated in
the houses of the Congregation from 1672, and this met with
great success. On this account St John Eudes deserves a very
high place in the history of Christian devotion.

To be complete, we ought to give the names of many others
who, each in his own way, continued to spread Bérulle's ideas.
As we should expect, the Oratory headed the list. The
Christological piety in which the Oratorians were trained
from their novitiate impregnated their thought and marked
even their most individual expressions. Nothing is clearer, for
example, than Bérulle's influence over Malebranche, and it
is a mistake to see that great philosopher as a pure metaphysician, when he is first and foremost an excellent devotional writer. The numerous books of devotion which sprang
from the Oratory spread among the faithful a simplified,
systematic Berullism, which gradually became part of the
spiritual air breathed by the seventeenth century. Thus even
before the middle of the century certain formulas and even
ideas of Berullism became common property in current use,
though the authors using them are not thereby Berullians.
A few decades ago, an author could be dubbed a Berullian
if he so much as spoke of the incarnate Word, but we realize
now we must be more guarded. St Vincent de Paul, for
instance, can hardly be considered a Berullian, though his

personal spirituality was in nowise original. It is the same with St John Baptist de La Salle, whose thought is very interesting and deserves to be better studied. As for Bossuet, he probably retained some traces of his reading of Bourgoing, but none of Bérulle's characteristic themes appear in his work, the sources of which are mainly patristic and scriptural. We shall return later to the problem of those Jesuits who are claimed as Berullians.

CHRISTOLOGICAL MYSTICISM

From what we have said it is clear that the Berullian current acted as an encouragement to mysticism. We can thus pass without any definite break from this group to another, which combined intense devotion to the incarnate Word with a more marked mystical tendency, a more special esteem for non-conceptual forms of prayer. These authors had various orientations. Some constructed in their own ways a synthesis between the ideas of the abstract school and those of Berullism; others, like the Jesuits, continued the line of Fr Lallemant, but expressed themselves with certain concessions to the prevailing Berullian climate.

Typical of this class is the famous Jean de Bernières-Louvigny (1602–59), treasurer-general of France. In 1646, with the help of another devout layman, Gaston de Renty, Bernières founded the retreat house of the Hermitage at Caen, which soon became the centre of a mystical group whose influence spread throughout Normandy. In this position he played the part of a real spiritual director, carrying on a large correspondence. It is rather hard to assess precisely the origin of his ideas. Through his own director, the Capuchin Chrysostom de Saint-Lô, he must have known the works of Canfield; through Renty, whose director was Condren, he must have been in touch with Berullism. On the other hand, several things suggest that he was familiar with both the Rheno-Flemish school and St Catherine of Genoa. At his death,

Bernières left behind him many writings, letters and notes on prayer, many of which long circulated in copies and were even then meant to be printed. Most unfortunately, his manuscripts are now irreparably lost and his thought is known to us only through very unreliable publications, composed out of it by not very scrupulous editors. Chief among them are the two volumes of the *Interior Christian* (1660 and 1677) and the *Spiritual Works* (1670), of which the latter seems nearer the original. Still, even through the medium of these transcriptions, certain lineaments of his thought can be discerned.

His longing for annihilation drives him to use the most absolute phrases expressing the "naughting" of Condren. In his mind, man has nothing of his own but contumely, abjection and nothingness. Bernières loves to dwell on this word "abjection", and to insist on the theocentric character of Christian devotion, in which God alone is all-sufficient. Like Fr de Condren, Bernières sees in Jesus himself the type and model of our abjection. The Incarnation is seen as a mystery in which God annihilates himself, and the humanity of Jesus gives itself to continual annihilations in order to enter the states of the divinity. He readily adopts the Berullian idea of adherence, but he means by this that we first enter into the states of abjection to which Jesus reduced himself in order to save us. By this absolute conformity to Jesus abject and despised, the soul should come to what Bernières calls the superhuman life, which recalls to some extent Canfield's supereminent life. Here, too, it involves a unitive state, in which the soul is perfectly abandoned to God. Further, Bernières recommended interior indifference, abandonment and pure love, in extremely trenchant words, which is no doubt why his works were put on the Index at the time of the Quietist crisis. His ways were those of mystical prayer and he urged his disciples on to passive contemplation with an insistence for which he was sometimes blamed by Marie des Vallées. All the same, notwithstanding their condemnation and their only moderate literary value, his works were often republished and for long found readers.

The Hermitage group and its many ramifications spread far and wide the influence of Bernières, whose memory continued to be venerated. Among his disciples mention should be made of the picturesque and hot-headed archdeacon of Evreux, Henri-Marie Boudon (1624–1702), and it is a pity that his eventful career has not yet attracted any scholar's pen. In the midst of all the innumerable rôles into which he was led by his reforming zeal, he found time to produce a very large volume of spiritual writings, in which the mysticism of Bernières was combined with the influence of St John of the Cross, whose life M. Boudon was one of the first to write in French.

Elsewhere, Bernières' influence was to some extent felt by two of the holiest nuns of the seventeenth century, with whom he was in touch: Marie de l'Incarnation and Mechtilde du Saint-Sacrement. The Venerable Marie de l'Incarnation (1599–1672) was born in Touraine and was called in the world Marie Guyart. In 1617 she married Claude Martin, by whom she had a son. Left a widow after about two years of married life, she soon began to experience exalted mystical states. She joined the Ursulines at Tours in 1630, and, as we know, went to Canada in 1639, where she was one of its apostles, combining unwearied activity with an intense contemplative life. Her son, who became a Benedictine under the name of Dom Claude Martin, was a spiritual writer of value and later became his mother's biographer. It is to his dutiful care that we owe many letters and various writings by Marie de l'Incarnation, especially two admirable autobiographical accounts composed in 1633 and 1654: on the authority of Bossuet himself these magnificent pages make the humble Ursuline seem a French Teresa. She analyses her interior states with almost astounding lucidity and candour. Her extremely lofty mysticism shows here and there the mark of the abstract school, but the influence of Bérulle, due no doubt to her relations with the Carmel at Tours and then with Bernières, is easily discerned. This accounts for the important place she gives in her spiritual life to the mysteries of Christ, and especially his Incarnation. Her works are therefore above all a self-revelation of a soul of exceptional quality, but the rich and solid doctrine they expound is a sort of mystical adaptation of Berullism.

The career of the Venerable Mechtilde du Saint-Sacrement (1614–98) was perhaps even more eventful. She was a Lorrainer, called Catherine de Bar, who became first an Annonciade Sister, then a Benedictine. Several times she had to flee the horrors of war and invasion and suffered much anguish and misery until in 1653 she founded the Benedictines of the Blessed Sacrament in Paris. Convents soon began to increase. Mother Mechtilde's foundation was indeed in the full stream of the devotion to the Eucharist, so intense in the seventeenth century. It made its appearance very soon, in reaction against the Calvinist denial of the real presence, and made it its task to offer reparation for outrages against the Blessed Sacrament. About 1631 there appeared the famous Company of the Blessed Sacrament, a secret society formed for this purpose, which soon, however, became a regular *cabale des dévots* and branched out everywhere, cooperating in a host of pious and charitable works. In 1626 Zamet, bishop of Langres, had thought of founding an Institute of the Blessed Sacrament, and in 1633 he had been able to realize his project with the help of Mother Angélique Arnauld, who had left her Abbey of Port-Royal for this purpose. The new congregation was short-lived, but in 1646 it was reassembled at Port-Royal, which was henceforth dedicated to the adoration of the Blessed Sacrament. However, the Benedictines of the Blessed Sacrament, supported by the devout *élite* of Paris and a very aristocratic group which included the queen, Anne of Austria, herself, extended their sphere of influence still further. It is against this background that Mother Mechtilde stands out so clearly: to the day of her death she never ceased to exert the influence of her peaceful, discreet mysticism. The greatest names of Catholic France are found in touch with her:

Bernières, Marie des Vallées, St John Eudes, Boudon, M. Olier, St Vincent de Paul, Bossuet, Fénelon and Mme Guyon. We still have a great number of her letters and various works of devotion, all admirable, but unfortunately for the most part unpublished. She shows herself faithful to Bernières' spirituality of annihilation and to the sacrificial ideas of Condren, and the personal synthesis she draws from them deserves really profound study.

In virtue of her contacts with Gaston de Renty, the Venerable Marguerite du Saint-Sacrement (1619–48), a Carmelite of Beaune, may be associated with the Caen circle. She was an ecstatic, who experienced the most extraordinary phenomena from childhood. In 1636, from the Carmel at Beaune, she began to propagate devotion to the Child Jesus. This, which originated in part from the work of Bérulle, rapidly attracted many followers. Marguerite du Saint-Sacrement is thus the source of a devotional current of considerable importance to the seventeenth century: it is well known what a large place the childhood of Jesus held in the piety of Fénelon and Mme Guyon. Finally, among the many mystics who grew to sanctity in the Carmels at this time, special mention must be made of the Venerable Madeleine de Saint-Joseph of Fontaines-Marans (1578–1637), first French Prioress of the Great Convent, whose outstanding holiness irradiated the whole world of the devout. An intimate confidante of Bérulle, she no doubt influenced the evolution of the great spiritual master, who had the highest esteem for her revelations and mystical states. Warmly attached to Berullian spirituality, she fought untiringly to defend it, to extend it in the Carmels and to lessen the influence of the abstract school. But her Berullism assumes a mystical form in many respects original and very attractive: it is a great pity that her writings, but for some very short fragments, have not yet been published.

In the same tradition should be mentioned Fr Louis Chardon (1595–1651), to our mind the most interesting of the French Dominican school of that time. In his day, however, he seems to have been almost unknown, and his masterpiece *The Cross of Jesus* (1647) met with little success: only in our own day has he come into his own. Chardon's doctrine is very rich. The centre of his interest is the analysis and explanation of the trials which pious souls meet on their path, and (though he does not call them so) it is the problem of passive purifications which he is facing. His descriptions of them reveal an uncommon degree of spiritual experience, but further, by means of the dogma of the mystical Body, he endeavours to construct a coherent theory of them. If sanctifying grace is participation in the very grace of Christ himself, it must needs make us enter into the suffering states of Christ, and the more intensely as the soul reaches a higher state of perfection: the mystical trials are thus set in direct relation with the Passion of our Lord. Chardon does not hesitate to use the systematic divisions of scholastic theology, but actually the influences to which he is subject are very complex. The most obvious is that of Canfield: for the Dominican, as for the Capuchin, the summit of the spiritual path is the supereminent life, where the soul attains to deifying transformation: Chardon's voluntarism is less marked, however, than Canfield's. His description of passive purifications owes much to Tauler, but some of his views on the Incarnation must be derived from Harphius. He may also have been somewhat influenced by Berullism. But for all that, the synthesis he devised is obviously original. Together with Chardon it is fair to mention another Dominican, Fr Alexandre Piny (1640–1709). He was a theologian, very faithful to Thomism, and his *Key of Pure Love* (1682) displays a voluntarism rather reminiscent of Canfield. But Piny wrote at a time when the victory of anti-mysticism was already on the way, and he did not venture to discuss openly certain states of the unitive life, a fact which limits his horizon.

The group of Jesuit spiritual writers presents some very complicated problems. It is difficult to see them as Berullians. The opposition between the Society of Jesus and the Oratory which persisted throughout the *ancien régime* is enough to make such a thing very unlikely. Even a cursory examination shows that none of the really original themes of Bérulle are found in their work; some modern commentators have made too much of some superficial analogies of vocabulary, particularly of the word "state", which had very soon become generally current. Should we style them, as some have done, the school of Fr Lallemant? It is doubtful. Everything leads us to think, as we have seen, that Fr Lallemant belongs to a tradition older than himself. Still, it is fair to note that many of Fr Lallemant's direct or remote disciples held an important place in the group, and it is to be desired that a serious critical study will succeed in deciding precisely what was the influence of this great teacher.

Specially characteristic is the case of Fr Jean-Baptiste Saint-Jure (1588–1657). There could really be no question of his being influenced by Fr Lallemant, with whom he was exactly contemporary: his thought is a remarkably well-constructed and original synthesis—yet the analogies it presents with that of Fr Lallemant are striking. In the *Spiritual Man* (1646) the praises he bestows on the northern mystics enable us to detect one important element of his inner world. But for him too, union with Jesus the incarnate Word constitutes a basic fact of the spiritual ways. Here he is in line with the Ignatian tradition, and he has certainly been influenced in this by Fr Antoine Le Gaudier (1572–1622), whose Latin treatises had already developed a very similar doctrine. Some have tried to see his work as an evolution in the direction of Berullism, but this seems scarcely tenable, for in 1634 Fr Saint-Jure had expressed his essential views in *The Knowledge and Love of the Son of God*, and had added little to them since then. Still he must have been to some extent affected by the Berullian vocabulary: in 1651, in fact, he wrote the biography of Gaston de Renty, friend of Bernières and disciple of Condren. Saint-Jure's works, sometimes of embarrassing abundance but teaching a discreet and measured mysticism, constitute a real summary of the Christian life which was the delight of the whole seventeenth century and was warmly recommended by Bossuet. So he witnesses to the existence of a stream in the Society of Jesus which comprises and surpasses Fr Lallemant.

Among Fr Lallemant's disciples a very special place belongs to Fr Jacques Nouet (1605–80), the master's intimate friend at Rouen and Bourges, who popularized his teaching in numerous works, of which the best known is *The Man of Prayer* (1674). We could wish, too, for a thorough study of the attractive Breton group. Here in particular we find Fr Jean Rigoleuc (1595–1638), whose notes were used, as we saw, to reconstruct Fr Lallemant's *Spiritual Doctrine*; Fr Vincent Huby (1608–93) and Fr Julien Maunoir (1606–83), who gave themselves with wonderful devotion to the work of missions and retreats. Also, though he belongs to the next generation, it would be unfair to omit Fr Pierre Champion (1631–1701), who became the editor and historian of this group, in which Fr Lallemant's tradition seems to have been very loyally preserved.

To the Breton group also belongs one of the most famous representatives of this tradition, Fr François Guilloré (1615–84), whose work is particularly important for the history of the spiritual movement. Its mystical aspect was very marked, so that in 1679 he incurred the bitter attacks of the Jansenist Nicole, and some suspicion at the time of the Quietist crisis. Guilloré is badly served by his clumsy style and often paradoxical expressions, for he is in fact a marvellous analyst of the inner life. He does not shirk undertaking the minute psychological dissections then in fashion, but he does so with a constant care to teach his disciple to transcend analyses, to forget himself and lose himself in God. Guilloré's work is abundant and fills a large folio (in which he took care, in 1684, to insert his best productions), but he often repeats himself, and his *Spiritual Maxims*, which appeared in 1668 with an approbation by St John Eudes, already contained the essentials of his thought. On the whole he agrees with Fr

Lallemant's ideas, and it was an exaggeration to make him out a Berullian on the strength of some mere similarities of vocabulary. But it is possible that he owes something to Condren and more to Séguenot, while other phrases recall Bernières. Like Lallemant, he attaches great importance to abandonment to the Holy Spirit, and he deduces from it a whole theory of spiritual direction, which in some ways reminds one of M. Olier. His mysticism, like Condren's, is above all one of annihilation, which in his eyes is the supreme homage of the creature to the Creator. It is in this setting of annihilation that he unerringly detects the obstacles which hinder the soul on its path to union, and to this problem he devotes what is without doubt the best of his works: *The Secrets of the Spiritual Life, Uncovering its Illusions* (1673). His analysis of mystical trials is extremely delicate and perhaps owes something to St John of the Cross. For him, as for Bernières, it is union with the self-abasement of the incarnate Word that sums up the way to God. It is easy to see the interest of this attractive work, which is only now beginning to be the subject of exact and critical study.

The rather unusual case of Fr Jean-Joseph Surin (1600–65) has long excited lively curiosity. Nothing in fact is more baffling than this mixture of evident sanctity with disturbing neuroses, in which some historians even now persist in diagnosing an element of diabolical influence. The aspect of him which interests us is not the certainly imprudent exorcist of the Ursulines of Loudun, but the spiritual writer. On this plane we cannot grudge our admiration, and his work remains one of the supreme achievements of devout literature in the French language. Unfortunately, it was published in precarious conditions and, except for some letters, we still await those critical editions which it so needs. Moreover, we must own that while Fr Surin has magnificence, a brilliant style, poetry and depth in his favour, in other respects the total absence of plan and a certain disorder in his thought are sad reminders that most of his books were written in the intervals between states of dementia. But at the time they were much admired in devout circles; many owe their printing to the Prince de Conti, and it was probably in deference to this aristocratic publisher that Bossuet gave his approval to the two most famous: the *Spiritual Catechism* (1661, already published in 1657) and the *Foundations of the Spiritual Life* (1667).

Fr Surin came under varied influences. A frequent visitor to the Carmel, he was an enthusiastic reader of St Teresa. In the course of his tertianship at Rouen in 1630, he was deeply affected by the prestige of Fr Lallemant. On the other hand, he was a great reader, and among his favourite authors the most important were Luis de la Puente, the northern mystics, St John of the Cross and St Catherine of Genoa. In addition, the part he played in the events at Loudun increased his rather morbid taste for abnormal phenomena. In details Fr Surin's thought sometimes lacks coherence, but there clearly emerge certain familiar themes, which connect him also with Fr Guilloré. He too insists on docility to the Holy Spirit, the inner teacher, and preaches that we must renounce our own lights. Similarly he is haunted by the idea of annihilation, and to effect this abnegation he advises union with Christ in his states of humiliation, in phrases which perhaps derive from his reading of Bérulle. He shows himself more original in the importance he attaches to the mystical forms of prayer, of which he rightly claims to find the type in St Ignatius himself. Finally, the central place he gives in his system to pure love makes him in many ways a precursor of Fénelon. A good monograph is needed to bring this attractive personality to life.

To complete these few lines on the great French spiritual masters of the Society of Jesus we should have to include many other names. In several of them we should find something of Fr Lallemant. It is interesting to note, for example, that an author like Fr Jean Crasset (1618–92), who in his *Meditations* (1678) and his *Method of Prayer* (1672) displays positively intellectualist tendencies, when it comes to his *Life of Madame Hélyot* (1683) can admirably describe and analyse the very abstract forms taken by his heroine's mental prayer. Lastly, we must mention the very lovable figure of Fr Claude de la Colombière (1641–82). The mistake is sometimes made of seeing him as simply the director of St Margaret Mary, but when he first knew her in 1675 he had long ago acquired his fundamental spiritual training. His profound knowledge of interior ways enabled him to understand the humble Sister of the Visitation better than anyone, and everything about him predisposed him to accept the revelation of the Heart of Jesus, on which such rich and beautiful passages had already been written by Fr Saint-Jure, Fr Nouet and Fr Crasset. It was in the posthumous publication of Fr de la Colombière's *Spiritual Retreat* that St Margaret Mary's secrets were revealed to the Christian world for the first time: but in addition the soul of this Jesuit is here revealed in its wonderful sanctity, mystical in form and very Ignatian, but echoing Fr Lallemant.

As for St Margaret Mary herself (1647–90), it is difficult to connect her with any school. Almost entirely self-taught, it seems, she was in no way a spiritual author. After her death, her Superior thought it better to burn almost all her writings, and those which survive were only published for the Sisters in 1867. Abstracting from the abundant commentaries devoted to them, we must admit that their doctrinal aspects are very limited, but the story of the great revelations is most moving. Her real importance lies, not in her writings, but in the great stream of devotion to the Sacred Heart which was to become so widespread in the eighteenth and nineteenth centuries. Of this she is one of the principal sources, though not the only source, as we have seen. It is a great pity that this devotion has been the occasion of so many writings burdened with polemical motives, which make objective history difficult. We may note by the way that the saint's idea of reparation bears some analogy with what is found at the same period in devotion to the Blessed Sacrament.

ABSTRACT MYSTICISM

All the authors we have just mentioned were to some extent affected by the abstract school, and it is only by very subtle differences that we can distinguish them from others whose tendencies link them more definitely with the tradition of Canfield. Throughout almost the whole century, in fact, Canfield remained an unchallenged master, and when, on account of the Quietist crisis, the *Rule of Perfection* was put on the Index in 1689 it made little difference, since the work went through four more editions, in 1694 and 1696. In this line of thought, some authors regarded the mystical life mainly from the angle of union with the divine essence and, without excluding Christ, were still attached to the idea of transcendence.

Of this group the most eminent representative was Jean de Saint-Samson (1571–1636), a Carmelite lay-brother belonging to the French reform of the Province of Touraine, which was different from the Teresan reform. Jean de Saint-Samson, who was blind, dictated throughout his career a body of mystical work which was rich and abundant, but diffuse and unsystematic. None of it had been published at the time of his death, and moreover the text was unpublishable, especially in that period. It was his fellow friar, Fr Donatien de Saint-Nicolas, who undertook to compile from these voluminous manuscripts the material for several publications, the whole of which appeared from 1654 to 1659. He performed the task in accordance with the customs of the time, not hesitating to retouch considerably the form as well as the matter, to dilute, explain away and tone down the blind man's abrupt and daring expressions. Thus, though the difference should not be exaggerated, there is a certain gulf between the real Jean de Saint-Samson and the bowdlerized version known to the seventeenth century. Through all this immense mass of badly classified writings it is often difficult to reconstruct the Carmelite's thought, which is not always quite coherent and on several points must have undergone development. His recommended reading enables us to identify his main sources, chief among them being Pseudo-Dionysius, Ruysbroeck and, above all, Harphius. To these he adds Tauler, the *Pearl of the Gospel*, St Catherine of Genoa and many other mystics. Besides these he had certainly read and used Canfield.

It is then chiefly on the northern mystics that Saint-Samson depends, and he holds to the line of their teaching. He too is a theorist on pure love, and divides it into active love and naked love. The latter, when perfectly stripped of all contact with the creature, introduces the soul to the mystical path and leads it to the supereminent life, at the cost of purifications which belong to the night of the soul, as described by St John of the Cross. It should be noted, however, that Saint-Samson hardly ever refers to St John, thinking, in fact, that he had never discussed the problems of the summit of the unitive life, and that there was still a state, higher than his most lofty descriptions. Saint-Samson, on the other hand, endeavours to analyse the final stages of the mystical union, the degrees of the supereminent life. He points out the purifying rôle of the fire of love in terms which recall the dark night of the soul. The soul surmounts these last degrees by entering the darkness, the mystical cloud, and here we meet the Dionysian influence. At the end, however, the soul passes out of this cloud to enter on a supreme, luminous stage—the stage of unbroken union, where it is totally consumed in its beatific object. Evidently Saint-Samson here agrees with Ruysbroeck. Further, he accepts one of the most daring themes borrowed by Ruysbroeck from Eckhart. For him, in fact, beings exist in God from all eternity, in their archetypes. This divine *idea* is deposited in man at the very centre of his soul. When man, by his movement of introversion, reaches his own centre, he *ipso facto* reaches his eternal archetype and loses himself in the divine essence, arriving at what Saint-Samson calls a final and supreme point of identification with God, a deiform deification. Because of the time of its publication and through its comparatively wide distribution, Saint-Samson's work played a very important part and contributed much to prolonging the influence of the Rhineland mystics.

With him should be associated another blind man, François Malaval of Marseilles (1627–1719), whose views are on a more moderate level, but belong to a similar world of thought. His *Easy Method for raising the Soul to Contemplation* (1664, enlarged edition in 1670) was given a very warm welcome and earned the praise of Fr Guilloré. Malaval offers to the humblest Christian a form of prayer which from the outset is mystical in type (at least inchoately) and which he calls the prayer of simple regard: it consists of a steady, loving gaze on God, present to us. Taking sides in a controversy which had agitated the theorists for some decades, Malaval distinguishes acquired contemplation from infused, and compares the prayer of simple regard to a real, acquired contemplation. This contemplation must be perfectly cut off from every image, every formulated thought, all interior discourse, in order to attain to God who is incomprehensible in himself. Here we can see how faithful Malaval is to the scheme of the abstract school and the Dionysian mystique of essences. But already, when this little book appeared, the anti-mystical reaction was growing. The *Easy Method*, vigorously attacked in 1687 by the Jesuit Ségneri, the opponent of Molinos, was put on the Index in 1688, and Bossuet, like Bourdaloue, later regarded the blind man of Marseilles as a precursor of Mme Guyon.

In his struggle against the authors he accused of Quietism, Nicole was quick to associate Malaval with the Premonstratensian Epiphane Louys, abbot of Etival († 1682). Dom Epiphane was the friend, and in many matters the adviser and supporter, of Mother Mechtilde du Saint-Sacrement. She prevailed upon him to give her Benedictines some courses of spiritual addresses which are found in *Mystical Conferences* (1676) and in several other works. These show the important part played by the Premonstratensians in the formation of the

nuns of the Rue Cassette. A champion of the prayer of simple
regard, like Malaval, Dom Epiphane here expounds a doctrine fairly near to his, but perhaps richer and more complete,
which deserves to be more studied. Some very interesting
Spiritual Letters of Dom Epiphane were published in 1688 by
another of his Order, his disciple Fr Michel La Ronde
(† 1718). Dom La Ronde is the author of a *Practice of the
Prayer of Faith* (1684) which was strongly criticized by
Bossuet in a letter to his disciple Mme d'Albert. This short
pamphlet, also published under the auspices of the Benedictines of the Blessed Sacrament, conforms to the ideas of Dom
Epiphane and also recalls Malaval. Fr La Ronde aims at
leading the soul to contemplate God as sovereign love and
universal truth, by a simple regard of the soul, together with
a loving tendency and inclination of the will. He quotes
copiously from Jean de Saint-Samson and Marie de l'Incarnation, but in fact he is steeped in the entire French mystical
tradition.

The fact is that the literature of mysticism continued to
flourish right up to the crisis of Quietism and gave birth to a
large number of works, whose authors are sometimes difficult
to identify. Some which have now fallen into oblivion were
very popular in their day. This was the case with the *Mystical
Day* (1671) by the Capuchin Pierre de Poitiers, which is
faithful to Canfield, but is also influenced by St John of the
Cross. Among this host of spiritual authors it is worth while
distinguishing the curious figure of Jean Desmarets de Saint-
Sorlin (1595–1676). He is best known as Richelieu's literary
collaborator, but in fact his activity as a spiritual writer
occupied an important part of his long career. It seems that
he must be regarded as the main author of the *Treatise on
the Perfection of the Christian*, which appeared in 1646 as the
posthumous work of Richelieu; it is possible that Desmarets
used the notes of Richelieu and Fr Joseph. Richelieu had
shown himself on the whole hostile to the representatives of
mysticism, whom he saw chiefly as political opponents; Fr

Joseph, after being definitely Canfieldian in his *Exercise of the Blessed* (1610), had come to share Richelieu's antipathies. When Desmarets published the *Treatise*, did he aim at serving the Cardinal's memory by showing that he had been no stranger to mysticism? It is true that it presents contemplation in a very restricted way, as a form of extraordinary prayer. His use of Thomist categories here and there suggests a Dominican influence, and it may perhaps be thought possible that he had the collaboration of Fr Carré, a Dominican, a friend of Fr Chardon and an agent of Richelieu. On the other hand there are some unmistakable borrowings from St Teresa and Canfield.

In works more definitely his own, Desmarets appears much more positively mystical. In 1661 he translated St Catherine of Genoa, with some success, but his major work in this connection is still *The Delights of the Spirit* (1658). It is a composite work, but very skilfully done. A first apologetic part, of Augustinian character, seeks to convert the freethinker by bringing him to find God in the "fine point" of the soul. This leads up to the second part, a treatise on contemplation, very markedly mystical, in which Desmarets perhaps owes something to his association with Boudon, who was a friend of his: in fact, the very obvious influence of St Teresa and St John of the Cross combines with that of the northern mystics and also of Bernières. In contemplation as he envisages it, the will alone acts, while the intellect loses all its light and remains as it were stupefied in the darkness, contemplating its object with the eyes of faith, not with its own, which no longer see anything. By his interference in the affairs of Port-Royal in 1664, Desmarets incurred the enmity of the Jansenists and the violent attacks of Nicole in his *Visionaries*, in which his spirituality itself was brought in question. But some ten new editions of his *Delights*, following each other up to 1691, testify to his enviable renown.

CHAPTER V

THE CRISIS OVER

MYSTICISM

ANTI-MYSTICISM

We have seen the tragedy that befell mysticism in sixteenth-century Spain and how the struggle against the *Alumbrados* hampered the greatest spiritual writers in their means of expression. The after-effects of this drama reached France in the seventeenth century, and here the conflict was more liberal in its development but more brusque and decisive in its conclusion. There very soon appeared in France a certain echo of the mistrust aroused by the mystics beyond the Pyrenees. For instance, while mysticism had some outstanding representatives among the Jesuits, it also encountered among them the liveliest resistance. In 1624 Fr Binet was railing against the "Dionysian balderdash", and we have seen that in 1629 the General, Mutius Vitelleschi, had to intervene against Fr Lallemant. Humanists and freethinkers alike scornfully mocked the mystics. At the same time many fervent Catholics thought this sort of piety to be dangerously illusory, and regarded the unitive states described by the Rheno-Flemish school and the Spaniards as sheer dreaming. They thought they should cling to the more solid and directly practicable way of asceticism and meditation. Mother Angélique Arnauld was thus very reserved about the extraordinary facts recorded in the life of St Teresa, and regarded the intellectual visions of Chancellor Marillac, reported to her by the Carmelites, as a mere diversion of the human mind. Even the Carmelite school left unexplored the path blazed by St John of the Cross, who had tried to assimilate the mysticism of the north, and confined themselves to the spirituality of St Teresa, interpreting it in a minimized sense. Jerome Gracian and Thomas of Jesus, two of the most illustrious men of the Order, urged on by the celebrated Anne of Jesus and by Brétigny, St Teresa's translator, found fault with the *Theologica Germanica* and indirectly with Canfield (1611). On their side, the Capuchins showed prudence. Though the *Rule of Perfection* appeared at Rouen in 1609, in its very daring original form, they hastened, as we saw, to produce official French and Latin editions in which the audacities were toned down. In such an atmosphere, the final decree against the *Alumbrados* published in 1623 by the Inquisitor Andrès Pacheco, and containing a list of seventy-six condemned propositions, had incredible repercussions. It was henceforth an arsenal providing anti-mysticism with its most powerful weapons for long to come. The *Mercure Français*, edited by Fr Joseph, published it in full: France may tolerate the Protestants, it implied, but Catholic Spain too has her heretics.

Richelieu's anti-mysticism, as we have seen, was coloured with political motives. All the same, various incidents during his period of absolute power helped to create a public opinion unfavourable to the mystics. There was, for example, the imprisonment of the Capuchin Laurent de Troyes, who had been expelled from his Order in consequence of disputes with Fr Joseph—though they were cousins. Having continued his preaching, which was much admired, he was finally arrested in 1629 and shut up in the Bastille, where he was kept in arbitrary imprisonment for thirteen years on a charge of Illuminism. Fr Joseph prevented his being tried by regular process of law, which would certainly have demonstrated the accused's innocence. Only Richelieu's death in 1642 restored him to freedom and rehabilitation. It is a curious fact that

Saint-Cyran, who had defended Laurent de Troyes, was himself under suspicion of Illuminism after his internment in Vincennes in 1638, and the same imputation was repeated in 1644 by Abra de Raconis, bishop of Lavaur, in his *Examination and Criticism of the Book on Frequent Communion*. The curiosity aroused by these incidents prompted the publication of various anti-mystical pronouncements, in particular *The Abomination of Abominations of the false Devotions of these Times*, by the Capuchin Archange Ripault (1631) and the anonymous *Letter from Agathon to Erastus* (1642), in which the Spanish and northern authors were indiscriminately attacked.

No less interesting is the strange affair of the Guérinets, or the Illuminists of Picardy, which was going on at the same time. The principal accused was Pierre Guérin, parish priest of St Georges de Roye; with him were implicated his two followers, the brothers Claude and Antoine Bucquet, together with the members of a little community of teaching nuns founded by the three priests at Roye and later known as the Daughters of the Cross. Judging by his book *The Holy Economy of the Family of Jesus* (1633) and by his constitutions for the Daughters of the Cross, Pierre Guérin appears to have been an adept of the abstract school, perfectly orthodox and a good disciple of Canfield, whose works he recommended for reading. It is hard to see what precisely were the reasons which in 1628 induced the Capuchins, headed by Fr Joseph, to attack the Guérinets, though it is true that some time before, during a visit to Montdidier, Laurent de Troyes had been in touch with the group at Roye. In 1630 two of the Daughters of the Cross succeeded in obtaining a statement in their favour signed by seventeen Paris theologians, but that did not check Fr Joseph's attacks. Guérin and the Bucquet brothers were arrested, imprisoned in the ecclesiastical courthouse at Amiens, then in 1644 transferred to the Bastille. A portion of the information laid against them still survives. It shows that there was an attempt to accuse them of the errors condemned in the *Alumbrados* by the decree of 1623, but contains not a shadow of evidence—for the fact, admitted by the accused, that they had read Canfield, Ruysbroeck, Tauler, St Catherine of Genoa and St John of the Cross, can hardly be considered a crime. In the end, after an enquiry conducted by St Vincent de Paul, who testified to their innocence, the accused were purely and simply discharged and reinstated in their functions; this solves the problem as far as we are concerned.

Mixed up in the Guérinet affair was an Augustinian nun of the Hôtel-Dieu at Montdidier, of which Antoine Bucquet was administrator. She was called Madeleine de Flers, and experienced very exalted mystical states, for which she was widely venerated. She had been arrested in 1629 and questioned by Fr Joseph himself and by André Duval; no charge had been laid against her and she had been released. During the summer of 1632 Dom Maugier, abbot of La Charmoye and superior of the Cistercian nuns of Maubuisson, had begged her to visit this latter abbey, where a group of young nuns desired to be introduced to mystical spirituality. They had been urged to it by their confessor, Dom Louis Quinet, later abbot of Barbery, who for his part was entirely in favour of the tendencies of the abstract school. The group met with the declared opposition of the abbess, Marie des Anges Suireau, a former religious of Port-Royal and trained by Mother Angélique in an essentially ascetic spirituality. In April 1631 Marie des Anges had succeeded in getting rid of Dom Louis Quinet and was far from enthusiastic over the arrival of Madeleine de Flers. Reading between the lines of all the malicious accounts which have come down to us through Jansenist sources, we can guess that Madeleine's teaching corresponded to the well-known themes of the abstract school, presented with perhaps more skill than prudence. The Augustinian was accused of turning the heads of the nuns, one of whom believed herself, or perhaps pretended, to be possessed by a devil. Madeleine was afraid she would be accused of sorcery and departed for Montdidier after a stay of about six months at Maubuisson, while in the following summer (1633) Saint-Cyran came to spend some months at the royal abbey to calm their minds. Madeleine de Flers escaped from the affair without further harm, except for another imprisonment in 1634, at the time of the last attack on the Guérinets.

As we can see, anti-mysticism was very soon represented in the Port-Royal circle. In the time of Saint-Cyran, however, there was no unanimity about it. It was by vindicating the relative freedom of expression of the mystics that in 1634 Saint-Cyran defended against Fr Binet the *Private Chaplet of the Blessed Sacrament* by Mother Agnès Arnauld, a little book full of Fr Condren's spirituality of annihilation, which by some complicated intrigues had been referred to the Sorbonne. But it is characteristic of the time that, in order to establish the orthodoxy of Mother Agnès' "naughting", Saint-Cyran represents it as emanating from St Augustine, and not, as it really was, continuing the Neoplatonism of the Rheno-Flemish school. But very soon, at Port-Royal as elsewhere, the mystics were compelled to beat a retreat.

SPIRITUAL PSYCHOLOGISM

From the middle of the seventeenth century the position of the mystics became year by year more critical, in spite of an apparent vitality, proved, as we have seen, by numerous publications. More and more it was the very movement of ideas that affected mysticism, depriving it of all reality and relegating it to the rank of an outmoded illusion. The mystics themselves, wrapped up in their own world, were no doubt blind to this process, which was actually more dangerous than open opposition, but their position was precarious and it only needed a shock to precipitate a crisis. It was the age when French piety was being invaded by psychology and intellectualism. The causes were legion. Cartesianism, whose triumph was steadily approaching, no doubt developed the taste for rational introspection, but from the dawn of the century there had begun to appear that passionate curiosity about what they called the human heart, the itch to take its most subtle mechanisms to pieces and to analyse the secret motives of men's acts. The most obvious results of this were of course in the field of literature, but it also affected spirituality where, too, the patronage of illustrious names helped to support it: we have only to think, for example, of the place occupied by psychology in the direction of St Francis de Sales. Towards 1660, many authors were coming to see the Christian life more and more from the angle of moralism, and the word "moral" began to figure in the titles of countless pious works.

This psychology was deliberately anti-mystical. Its passion for reason, analysis and logical clarity made it hostile on principle to a spirituality which tended to place prayer beyond conceptual and discursive forms and to lose itself in the irrational and unformulated elements of Dionysian darkness. Without denying the existence of the mystical ways, guaranteed by the lives of so many saints, it was unwilling to see them as anything but miraculous and exceptional facts, unrelated to the ordinary spiritual life. By and large, it distrusted everything except clear and reasoned consciousness. The moralists of the *salon*, we know, accepted almost as an article of faith the idea of La Rochefoucauld, that man is by nature turned towards himself, that self-love is the principle, the spontaneous motive, of his actions and reactions. The spiritual moralists adopted the theme with glee, and without realizing their unconscious contradiction took it as an illustration of St Augustine's views on the contrast between self-love and the love of God. Here they agreed to some extent with the mystics, who had never ceased to preach the renunciation of self-love, but where the mystics saw no solution save transcending it by complete forgetfulness of self, the moralists prescribed a whole course of therapy, based on self-knowledge and introspection, lucid, minute and pitiless. Hence their particular brand of moralism, steeped in psychology and darkened with pessimism. On the other hand, all-embracing as were their moral preoccupations, they did not lack dogmatic solidity, and on this point many of them were full in the Christological current which continued Berullism while simplifying it.

When we speak of spiritual psychologism, the first name which comes to mind is that of Pierre Nicole (1625–95), a native of Chartres, well known by his rôle in the Jansenist party. After his break with Arnauld in 1679 he devoted himself almost entirely to writing books of spirituality; already in 1672 he had begun to publish those *Essays in Morality* of which the last volumes are posthumous. Their popularity for more than a century is well known, and proved by more editions than one can count. It is true that later generations made him pay dearly for it, and the Essays are now buried in unmerited oblivion. Nicole's style is sometimes rather heavy, but his superiority is affirmed by the depth of his thought and the wealth of his theological knowledge. The precision of his analyses, which so charmed Mme de Sévigné, hardly introduced any new elements on the spiritual plane. In this respect Nicole interests us chiefly because he was, dare we say, a militant anti-mystic, and for this he bears a heavy responsibility. His rigorous intellectualism is hermetically sealed and he tends to reduce the inner life to nothing but conscious and discursive thought. He admits contemplative prayer in theory and asserts his respect for the works of St Teresa and St John of the Cross, but in them he sees God's special conduct with certain privileged souls, rather than the ordinary road by which God makes the common run of Christians to enter, and he insists on the exceptional and transitory nature of these states. In many cases, too, he refuses to see anything in passive prayer but a sheer illusion of human origin. His intellectualism makes him the champion of meditation and methodical prayer and rebels against the tendencies of the abstract school: to drive out of the mind all thoughts, good or bad, to think no more about the humanity of Christ or his mysteries, seems to him something monstrous, contrary both to the doctrine of the Fathers and to the good of souls. Hence his hostility to the prayer of simple regard, which he says is to blame for the worst aberrations. Relying on these principles, which were reinforced by an unshakable inability to understand the opposite type of thought, Nicole continued till his dying day to fight the mystics, and his last work was a *Refutation of the Errors of the Quietists* (1695) in which he named Molinos, Mme Guyon, Dom Epiphane Louys and Malaval. But he had opened the battle in 1679 with the publication of his *Treatise on Prayer*, in which he claimed to refute Bernières, Guilloré and Barcos. The last-named, nephew of Duvergier de Hauranne, and, like him, abbot of Saint-Cyran, had a curious and original position. One hesitates to call him a mystic, for he rejected what is the fundamental idea of mysticism, the possibility of an experience of the divine. But he advocated abandonment to the inner guidance of the Holy Spirit and rebelled against all methods of prayer which, he said, claimed to make rules for the action of God and to subject him to our ways. In this, Barcos believed himself to be in agreement with the practice of the primitive saints and took little account of the authority of the moderns, even of St Francis de Sales. Such an attitude, naturally incurred the vigorous disapproval of Nicole and even of Antoine Arnauld.

On the other hand spiritual psychologism has enriched our Christian literature with some remarkable books, sometimes unfairly forgotten, which it is difficult to describe justly in a short summary. For their value lies in the detail of their wonderfully industrious research and in the settled balance of the piety they present. Many names might here be mentioned. In particular we could not omit that of M. Louis Tronson (1622–1700), the third superior-general of Saint-Sulpice. Tronson was rightly considered one of the holiest priests of his time. But the way in which he edited and sometimes interpreted M. Olier shows his distaste for mysticism, while his psychological bias is shown in his famous *Particular Examinations* (1690), a masterpiece which has trained many generations of priests in introspection, though unfortunately it has been spoiled by emended editions. In the same stream we should include the Oratorian Pasquier Quesnel (1634–1719), well known for his activity as leader of the Jansenist party, but he was also a very fertile devotional writer. Incidentally, it was one of his works of devotion, his *Moral Reflections on the New Testament* (first edition, 1671, with the title *The Morality of the Gospel*, complete edition, 1693) which occasioned the conflicts involving the Bull *Unigenitus*. Quesnel's spirituality is much more rational and dogmatic than psychological and is deeply imprinted with Berullism. His works had an amazing circulation in the eighteenth century, even beyond Jansenist circles, and it is interesting to note that apart from the *Moral Reflections* none of his books of piety were put on the Index. In his famous *Christian Prayers* (1687), so often reprinted, and in his *Devotion to Jesus Christ* (1696) his Berullism finds expression, but moralism triumphs in the three volumes of a *Collection of Spiritual Letters on Divers Subjects of Morality and Piety* (1721–3), which contain some fine passages, showing that Fr Quesnel was a penetrating director. The Jesuit Louis Bourdaloue (1632–1703) is chiefly famed for his preaching, but he was also a noted confessor, and might have been a remarkable spiritual writer if his crushing labours had left him time for it. Unfortunately, his work is almost all posthumous and was published in rather dubious conditions. He shows his mastery of a very supple and penetrating psychology, but towards mysticism he betrays a mistrust which is tainted with hostility.

It is arguable that moralism produced its finest flower in the Jansenist Jacques-Joseph Du Guet (1649–1733). We are not concerned with the polemical aspect of his career, and in any case the greater part of his work deals with spirituality. His printed works exceed a hundred volumes, and this abundance which so delighted the eighteenth century discourages modern readers. Even so, on the merely literary plane, Du Guet deserves to be revived, for he is an admirable writer, whose only fault is the too even perfection of his style. His Oratorian formation accounts for the presence in his work of many themes of Berullian inspiration, especially in his voluminous *Treatise on the Cross of our Lord Jesus Christ, or, an Explanation of the Mystery of the Passion* (1733). Nonetheless, his inspiration often comes from a very profound knowledge of the Fathers; from them he draws well-balanced counsels of piety, in which a strict moralism, tainted with Jansenist austerity, is tempered with a very keen sense of the presence of God and of adoration. His famous *Treatise on Public Prayer* (1707), written for Gillot (a canon of Rheims who complained of the length of the offices), is certainly a model of this type of work. But it is in psychological analysis that Du Guet chiefly reveals himself in all his finesse and depth: of this there are many perfect examples in the ten volumes of *Letters on Divers Subjects of Morality and Piety* (1707–53). Du Guet was little interested in mysticism, but he was not so hostile to it as might be supposed. At one time he was even interested in a rather questionable mystic, Catherine d'Almayrac, known as Sister Rose.

Together with Du Guet we may mention another Jansenist, no less devoted to Sister Rose, Jean-Jacques Boileau, or Beaulaigue, to give him his real name (1649–1735), known from his functions under Cardinal Noailles as M. Boileau de l'Archevêché. His *Letters on Different Subjects of Morality and Piety* (1737) are chiefly quoted because they contain the anecdote of Pascal and his abyss,[1] but they are very interesting for other reasons and are connected with the same tendencies as Du Guet. As we see, the great Jansenist directors contributed powerfully towards the triumph of spiritual psychologism

[1] He said that in consequence of an accident to the brain Pascal always thought he saw an abyss on his left side. See J. Chevalier, *Pascal* (Plon), p. 101.

which occurred in the eighteenth century, and specially in France. Other less-known names belonging to the same trend also deserve mention, since they were largely responsible for the over-rigorous moralism which often darkened the piety of this age. Jérôme Besoigne (1686–1763), best known as the historian of Port-Royal, is also the author of many works of devotion, whose dogmatic solidity does not, unhappily, compensate for their intolerable dryness. The same might be said of René Cerveau (1700–80), famous for his *Necrology of the Appellants*, a worthy disciple of Nicole and Quesnel, but cold and formal. All this discouraging literature was a sign that French spirituality was on its deathbed.

THE QUIETIST CRISIS

In spite of Nicole's efforts, the mystics for long had many supporters and it was only in the last years of the century that things came to a crisis. The signal was given at Rome by the complicated business which arose over the Spaniard Miguel Molinos, in 1685. This man had been for many years a highly approved spiritual director and in 1675 had published, with the highest approbations, his *Spiritual Guide*, largely inspired by St John of the Cross and the Rhineland mystics, when he was accused of the gravest moral depravities. It is hard to define just how responsible Molinos was, or how far he was really involved in the erroneous spirituality which was given the name of Quietism: on all these points many modern historians are unwilling to commit themselves. In any case the ideas of Molinos had little response in France. The *Spiritual Guide* appeared first in Italian and was only translated into French in 1688, after his condemnation, in a series of Protestant origin. On the other hand, Molinos' trial made a great impression on public opinion, and even some Gallicans, like Talon, the advocate-general, took occasion to accuse Pope Innocent XI of indulgence towards the Roman Quietists. The decree of August 28th, 1687, condemning sixty-eight propositions attributed to Molinos, was immediately known and commented on in France. It gave fresh life to the decree against the *Alumbrados*, which was becoming a dead letter, and provided anti-mysticism with a plentiful choice of ready-made charges. But several years had still to pass before the affair came to a head.

The central character in this last scene was a woman, Jeanne-Marie Bouvier de la Motte (1648–1717). Left a widow in 1676 by Jacques Guyon du Chesnoy, who bequeathed her three children and a vast fortune, she resolved to dedicate herself to works of piety and charity. By this time she had already attained to mystical forms of prayer, under various influences which it is hard to assess with accuracy. One of them was certainly her director, Jacques Bertot († 1681), confessor to the Benedictines of Montmartre, who was a friend and disciple of Bernières and closely associated with Mother Mechtilde. His spiritual writings, which are very interesting, were published much later under the title of *The Mystical Director* (1726). Through Bertot, Mme Guyon was linked with the Caen group, to whom she owed several of her orientations. On the invitation of Mgr d'Arenthon, bishop of Geneva, she went to Gex to arrange for a foundation of "Nouvelles Catholiques";[2] then, having quarrelled with the bishop, she lived in Turin, Grenoble and Vercelli. In the course of the years she spent in Savoy, she had joined forces with a Barnabite, Fr François La Combe, who became her director and accompanied her on many of her journeys. Returning to Paris in 1686, she there continued the apostolate of mysticism to which she had devoted herself in the various towns in which she had stayed, and through which she had already been involved in different incidents. From January to September of 1688, a mysterious affair, whose roots were probably more financial than doctrinal, caused her to be interned with the Sisters of

[2] A community founded in 1634 by Archbishop de Gondi for Protestant young women about to enter the Church, or converts who needed to be strengthened in the Faith.

the Visitation. She was set free through the good offices of Mme de Maintenon, who introduced her to the royal House at Saint-Cyr. It was soon after this, in October 1688, that she made the acquaintance of Abbé de Fénelon, who likewise enjoyed Mme de Maintenon's good opinion and had the entrée to Saint-Cyr.

By this time Mme Guyon's thought was fully formed and she had composed her essential works. One of them had been fairly successful: the *Short and Easy Method for Prayer*, published at Grenoble in 1685 and soon several times reprinted. Mme Guyon was like Malaval in her endeavour to initiate the faithful to a very simple form of prayer which at once tends to mysticism. She called it the prayer of the heart, a term which seems to have been popularized by the Dominican Piny, who published a small book with this title in 1683. We must remember that, like all her contemporaries, she practically identifies heart, love and will. She invites the soul to turn and collect itself in its interior, in order to remain in continual adherence to God: this reminds us of the movement of introversion beloved of the Flemish mystics. The soul must keep silence in itself, suppressing all its own activity, in order to live in the presence of God, in abandonment and faith.

The teaching of the *Short and Easy Method* is on a comparatively elementary level, and to supplement it we must consult the earliest of Mme Guyon's writings, *The Torrents*, written in 1682, which until its publication in 1704 circulated in countless manuscript copies. The "torrents" are the mystical souls who are swept towards God by the vehemence of pure love, and seek him in the depths of their own being, without leaving themselves. They pass through the bitterness of passive purifications, described by Mme Guyon with extreme precision, through which they are led to a state of death and annihilation. Beyond this stage these souls are raised up again, being clothed in the state of all the inclinations of Christ, and so become one with God, losing themselves in the divine essence by a pure and general contemplation which has no object and no distinctness. Thus in the end Mme Guyon rejoins abstract mysticism, but in the place she gives to Christ the influence of Bernières is easily recognized: on the other hand she has been considered a remarkable interpreter of St John of the Cross. During her stay in Grenoble, in 1684, she wrote with incredible rapidity a mystical commentary on the Bible; of this enormous work only the *Canticle of Canticles* was at first published, at Lyons in 1688. It contains some fine passages, but its rather garrulous prolixity, though less disordered than is alleged, adds nothing of substance to the *Short and Easy Method* and the *Torrents*. With Mme Guyon's writings should be compared a slender Latin work by Fr La Combe, which appeared at Vercelli in 1686, *Orationis mentalis analysis* ("An analysis of mental prayer"), an interesting attempt to defend Mme Guyon's principles with the support of theological authorities. During the anti-mystical reaction which followed the Molinos affair at Rome, when condemnations were launched against authors hitherto most highly esteemed, the *Analysis* was put on the Index, along with the *Short and Easy Method*: but this was the only one of Mme Guyon's works to be condemned at Rome.

When the brilliant young Abbé de Fénelon met Mme Guyon, he seems to have been going through a painful attack of aridity and emptiness in his inner life. Friendship between them soon became intimate and deep, and from now on he always reverenced her as a saint. The mysticism she taught him solved his personal problems. From letters they exchanged during 1689 we can see that she gradually brought him to understand that the reality of union with God is something far above all that is known or felt. She led him to establish himself in a state of non-seeing and indifference, to strive for complete oblivion of self. At this same time Fénelon read much, not only the mystical authors but the Fathers and the schoolmen, and thus acquired an uncommon degree of culture in this field. While to a great extent he preserved the independence of his thought, his own spirituality was being formed, nonetheless, in the Guyon atmosphere.

Among the Ladies of Saint-Cyr Mme Guyon's teaching made many converts, who were not always very discreet. There was malicious gossip outside, and Mme de Maintenon took note that her enemies were covertly formulating a terrible charge of Quietism against her and her foundation. To escape from this peril she first of all sacrificed Mme Guyon, who about March 1693 was requested to abandon her visits to the royal House. At the same time, with the help of her confessor Paul Godet des Marais, bishop of Chartres, Mme de Maintenon tried to neutralize Fénelon's influence in the house, as it reinforced that of Mme Guyon. Entreated both by Fénelon, who felt himself indirectly attacked, and by Mme Guyon, who wanted to ensure for herself some solid doctrinal support, Bossuet now took in hand the examination of her writings, in August 1693. He was in nowise qualified by his training for such a task; the few approbations he had granted to Surin or Boudon, probably out of courtesy, did not in any way prove him really competent. At first he seems to have been undecided, but the authority of Mme de Maintenon outweighed the friendship which already bound him to Fénelon. In March 1694 he gave a verdict which was positively unfavourable. He blamed Mme Guyon chiefly for her views on the passive state and pure love, which seemed to him to do away with the exercise of the Christian virtues and the prayer of petition. If some of his criticisms are justified by her often vague phrases, Bossuet showed himself very lacking in understanding of mysticism, which he would fain have reduced to a few cases quite outside the normal paths. As slanderous rumours continued to circulate, Mme Guyon asked to be officially examined on her faith and morals.

Mme de Maintenon having consented, the Issy Conferences were organized to this end, and from July 1694 they brought together, in the country house of the Saint-Sulpice seminary, M. Tronson, Bossuet and Antoine de Noailles, bishop of Châlons, who in August 1695 was transferred to the see of Paris. Without being a member of the commission, Fénelon took part in it by sending several memoranda. The most remarkable is a writing on the passive state, in which he shows that this is identical with holy indifference as described by St Francis de Sales, and also with pure love or perfectly disinterested charity. Already we can recognize Fénelon's personal tendency to systematize the whole problem in terms of pure love. He resumed the same ideas in a much more considerable work, *The Gnosticism of St Clement of Alexandria*. This is an acute and penetrating study in which he claims to discover in the "gnosis" of Clement the mystical state of modern authors. Bossuet replied with his *Tradition of the New Mystics*, in which the same texts are given an exaggeratedly minimal interpretation. Naturally, all these essays remained in manuscript. Being nominated in February 1695 to the archbishopric of Cambrai, Fénelon was able to take part in the final deliberations, and to take a hand in drawing up the thirty-four Articles of Issy, which in conclusion were signed by the prelates and M. Tronson. In its main lines the text of the Articles was due to Bossuet, who displayed therein a rather narrow intellectualism, but some concessions to the mystics were extorted by Fénelon. Some time later, in his correspondence and in various writings, Fénelon imposed so forceful an interpretation on the Articles of Issy that he found his own spirituality in them. Bossuet and Noailles, on the contrary, used them in April 1695 to obtain Mme Guyon's official condemnation. Mme de Maintenon had hoped that Fénelon would do the same in his diocese of Cambrai, but he refused point blank, holding such an action incompatible with the veneration he felt for Mme Guyon. Mme de Maintenon was very angry at this: she had hoped at least that Fénelon would give his approval to the lengthy pastoral instruction being prepared by Bossuet, in which Mme Guyon would be refuted. On July 23rd, 1696, the manuscript was sent to Fénelon, who after a cursory inspection gave a no less categorical refusal, and Bossuet shared in the anger of the king's wife.

Fénelon realized that conflict was inevitable, and he must hasten to take up his positions. Making use of the vast body of documents he had collected at the time of the Issy Conferences, during the summer of 1696 he wrote at Cambrai his *Explanations of the Maxims of the Saints on the Interior Life*. Afraid lest Bossuet might succeed in preventing his book being published, he let his friends hurry on the printing of it and finally, through their zeal, anticipated Bossuet: the *Maxims of the Saints* was released to the public in February 1697. To be frank, it was scarcely a book for the ordinary reader. Its presentation was dry and hard, its formulas too unqualified. After an explanatory preface and the text of the Articles of Issy, Fénelon expounds and analyses the five states of love, distinguished by their degree of disinterestedness. They run from servile love to pure love and mark out the purgative, illuminative and contemplative ways: he thus clearly proclaims, from the start, his theory of mysticism built on the idea of pure love. Then follow forty-five articles, summing up the principal points of spiritual theology; for each, Fénelon explains its true sense and excludes possible false interpretations. In his original draft he had supported these with quotations from the most approved authors, but on Noailles' advice he lightened his book by omitting these authorities, which was certainly a mistake. On many points, Fénelon's mysticism seems more moderate than that of the abstract school, whose Neoplatonic themes, in any case, he passes over in silence. Thus Article 27, on the exclusion of images in contemplation, rejects as false some ideas which were certainly defended by several representatives of the abstract school. Similarly, his views on transformation in God are much less bold than Canfield's manner of envisaging deiformity in the supereminent life. On the other hand, Fénelon is certainly wrong in giving undue importance to the problem of indifference to salvation, which he does not present well.

The public's welcome to the *Maxims of the Saints* was at

first somewhat undecided, and Fénelon found many supporters among the Jesuits, the Dominicans and the Oratorians.
After a few days of suspense, Bossuet began to stir up opinion
and to put the king against Fénelon, now openly accused of
Quietism. In March 1697, more than a month behind his
rival, he produced his *Instruction on the States of Prayer*. It
is a stout volume, polemical, developed at length, logical in
plan and rhetorical in form, far more to the taste of the day
than Fénelon's arid *Maxims*. But the scornful way in which
Bossuet speaks of Ruysbroeck, Harphius and even St John
of the Cross, makes one wonder: by refusing to consider the
data of mystical experience as they actually happened in great
religious personalities, he makes insoluble a problem which
cannot be treated from *a priori* considerations of theory alone.
By confining the mystical state to a small number of miraculous cases he compels himself to view the Christian life from
a narrow and absurdly restricted angle. To be frank, the
Instruction is a work of incomplete and often debatable
doctrine. But it matched the prejudices of the moment, and
its success helped to put the unfortunate Fénelon, champion
of a now lost cause, in an impasse. Afraid of being condemned
by the Assembly of the Clergy, Fénelon twice appealed from
it to Rome, on April 27th and August 2nd, 1697, and his
appeal was supported by Louis XIV. Now the fight went on
simultaneously in Paris and in Rome, where Fénelon was
represented by the worthy if rather naïve Abbé de Chantérac,
and Bossuet by his nephew, the unscrupulous Abbé Bossuet.

The battle in Paris was fought on three fields. On that of
spirituality there were many points of controversy, but two
in particular claim our attention. First, that of the passive
state, which Bossuet persisted in regarding as a miraculous
ligature of the powers of the soul, while to Fénelon it was
nothing but total, peaceful and gentle cooperation with grace
and the divine action. Here, in fact, two opposed conceptions
of the mystical life confront each other: the one which regards
it as a quite special and exceptional grace, the other which

considers it simply as the prolonging and full flowering of the
sanctifying grace common to all Christians. Second, there
was the problem of indifference to one's own salvation, connected with the absolute disinterestedness of the mystics and
also with the "sacrifice of salvation" in certain interior trials.
On this point, the debate led Fénelon to modify the rather
rigid positions of the *Maxims*. In all this, Fénelon gave proof
of a wide spiritual culture which was lacking in his opponent:
it is typical, for example, that all Fénelon's quotations from
St John of the Cross were authentic, with hardly an exception,
while Bossuet's were almost entirely spurious, interpolated by
the editors. Here Fénelon had no trouble in showing that his
positions were solidly based on tradition.

On the field of theology the battle centred round pure love.
To Bossuet, charity must always involve an interested aspect,
a certain search for God as one's private beatitude. Fénelon
states, on the contrary, that charity, to be perfect, must also
be perfectly disinterested, seeking none but God alone, for
himself, with no thought of self. Fénelon here made the mistake of becoming involved in secondary problems, especially
that of how the virtue of hope can be reconciled with pure
love. But there is no doubt that his opinion had the support
of most of the Fathers and the Schoolmen. In his remarkable
pastoral instruction of September 15th, 1697, he developed his
views in a very accurate manner which satisfied many experts.
Here again, Bossuet could not hope in any way for a decisive
victory.

On the doctrinal level, then, the struggle was undecided. It
was a sorry stroke of genius on Bossuet's part to move it on
to the plane of personalities, by methods which make him
the father of a certain type of journalism. In June 1698
appeared the famous *Relation on Quietism*, a bitter pamphlet,
in which no fundamental question was discussed, but Mme
Guyon was represented as a half-mad visionary, and Fénelon,
in so many words, as the Montanus of this Priscilla. Bossuet
did not scruple to make use of the most intimate confidences,

quoting at length from an autobiographical memoir drawn up by Mme Guyon for her director under the seal of secrecy, and publishing in full a private letter to her from Fénelon. Such proceedings amounted to defamation. But they were sadly effective, and Fénelon's noble reply, which appeared in the following August, only partially restored the situation. Further, Bossuet had hoped to intensify his campaign with still more scandalous accusations. Mme Guyon, arrested and imprisoned in December 1695, was again submitted to questioning and minute police inquiries, in the hope of compromising her as well as Fénelon; it is tragic to see Bossuet so lowering himself as to take La Reynie, lieutenant of police, as his assistant and informer. However, it was in vain, and Mme de Maintenon and Bossuet had their trouble for nothing.

Rome, for its part, at first hesitated. Bossuet, a Gallican and known as the author of the famous Four Articles of 1682, had to reckon with foes as well as friends, while Innocent XII hardly concealed his sympathy for Fénelon, who was more favourable to the Holy See. Very important groups, especially the Jesuits, did not grudge their support for the archbishop. The theologians of the commission charged with examining the *Maxims of the Saints* were also divided, and for a long time the pope thought that they could not condemn Fénelon without at the same time attacking St Teresa. However, the publication in Rome of the *Relation on Quietism* was very damaging to Fénelon, and many then thought that his cause was seriously compromised. Even so, perhaps, the clever intrigues of Abbé Bossuet might not have carried the day but for the personal intervention of Louis XIV, who was entirely on Bossuet's side and put the formidable weight of his authority in the balance.

The disasters which befell Fénelon, his family and friends showed where the king stood, and thinly-veiled threats put pressure on the Roman Curia, gradually leading the cardinals to pronounce against the *Maxims*. Finally Innocent XII gave in, but instead of the Bull in solemn form which had been

expected he only gave a brief, and that with the clause *motu
proprio* ("on his own initiative"), which the French Parliament
only accepted with difficulty. The brief *Cum alias* was signed
on March 12th, 1699; it condemned, in terms as mild as
possible, twenty-three propositions taken from the *Maxims
of the Saints*. Not one of the numerous documents Fénelon
had written for his defence was attacked. In an episcopal
charge dated April 9th, Fénelon submitted unreservedly to
this sentence, an act which won for him an exceptionally
complimentary brief from Innocent XII. A little later, about
October, the pope showed his true sentiments by making
Fénelon a Cardinal. Altogether it does not seem that this
condemnation changed much in Fénelon's thought or sympa-
thies. After a long captivity, Mme Guyon emerged from the
Bastille in March 1703 and was exiled to Blois, where she
continued her mystical apostolate. To the end of his life
Fénelon preserved his attachment to the woman who had, all
involuntarily, ruined his career.

Innocent XII was right. Fénelon had made himself the
champion of the mystics; in an already hostile public opinion
the condemnation which fell on him struck at mysticism itself,
and the brief *Cum alias* sounded its retreat. The eighteenth
century saw the almost complete rout in France of Catholic
mysticism, which without completely disappearing remained
concealed. The same period witnessed the triumph of spiritual
psychologism which, as we have seen, flourished and then fell
back on itself. Deprived of the living source of inner experience, the literature of devotion went on drying up, retain-
ing no more than a distant memory of the magnificent
flowering it had known on French soil. A precious product,
but a little frail and over-refined, the fruit of complex influences, this French spirituality came in the Age of Reason
to the end of its history.

There were still, even so, a few very cautious attempts to
give French devotion the appearance of life. Some authors,
without trying to restore even the most moderate ideas of

mysticism, kept at least the affective style which expresses the prayer of the heart. Such was the Minim Jean-Baptiste-Elie Avrillon (1652–1729), whose considerable output, largely posthumous, is unfortunately not free from pious sentimentality. But he had the excellent idea of seeking inspiration from Marguerite du Saint-Sacrement in order to write some fine passages on the Childhood of Jesus. The Capuchin Ambroise de Lombez (1708–78) was deservedly successful with his *Treatise on Interior Peace* (1757), in which a very penetrating moralism is touched with a vague suggestion of mysticism. We should be to blame if we did not mention here St Louis-Marie Grignon de Montfort (1673–1716), one of the most extraordinary and attractive figures of Christian sanctity in the dawn of the eighteenth century. His brief career was consumed in an ardent apostolate which scarcely left him time for spiritual writing. Still, he did not lack talent, but after his death his manuscripts were buried in oblivion, and his two great works were not published till the nineteenth century: *The Love of the Uncreated Wisdom* (1876) and above all the *Treatise on True Devotion to the Blessed Virgin* (1842), which gives expression to his deep devotion to our Lady. A follower of Bérulle and his vow of servitude, Montfort is obviously steeped in Oratorian spirituality, but he borrows from other forerunners. His cult of the eternal Wisdom, for example, comes to him from Suso, the last of the Rheno-Flemish school still to be read in France: as late as 1684 a translation of his *Dialogue on the Eternal Wisdom* had appeared, dedicated to Bossuet. Here, too, we wish that the problem of Montfort's sources could be critically studied.

Other authors did their best to recall the attention of the faithful to mysticism, now unhappily fallen into almost universal disrepute. It was the Jesuits who thus remained faithful to the great spiritual tradition, while simplifying it as much as possible. Of this group, two are still well known, and first, Fr Jean-Pierre de Caussade (1675–1751). As a director of the Visitation Sisters, Fr de Caussade found himself in touch with a *milieu* in which mysticism was still a living thing, and he must have had to face the problem. From his reflections emerged the *Spiritual Instructions in the form of a Dialogue on the different States of Prayer, according to the Teaching of M. Bossuet* (1741). Rightly observing that in his practice of direction the bishop of Meaux had proved far more favourable to mysticism than might have been expected, Fr de Caussade drew from the *Instruction* of 1697 a complete theory of the interior life, of a type on the whole very like Fénelon's. Along with this he published a curious *Short and easy Method of making Mental Prayer in Faith and the simple Presence of God*, which the Visitation Sisters had shown to him as a work of Bossuet's, an attribution which needs closer examination. This ingenious and paradoxical plea does not seem to have met with great success. Then there was Jean-Nicolas Grou (1731–1803) who, after the dissolution of the Society of Jesus, went to end his days in England, where he wrote most of his books. He has provided many souls, down to our own day, with spiritual nourishment of a high order, which reproduces certain aspects of the spirituality of Lallemant. In spite of this he was not successful in restoring mysticism to its former place, now that public taste had so rejected it. In 1775 M. Emery, a future superior-general of Saint-Sulpice, brought out a *Spirit of St Teresa* in which, to accommodate the work of the great Carmelite to the taste of the times, its mystical element is almost entirely eliminated.

MYSTICISM IN EUROPE

If France holds only a minor place in the earlier part of this work, she clearly dominates the rest. It was in fact in France that spiritual ideas were able to develop with the greatest freedom and breadth, and that was where the most important part of their destiny was worked out. During the sixteenth century France had lived on importations and translations, but thenceforth the exchange was in the other direction. Numerous books by French authors were sent abroad and spread their message afar. The *Introduction to the Devout Life*, for example, appeared in Italian in 1610, in English in 1613, in German and Spanish in 1616. Canfield's *Rule of Perfection* was translated into Italian in 1616, Dutch in 1622, Spanish in 1628 and German in 1633. Latin translations abounded for the use of theologians; even Jean de Saint-Samson was so favoured in 1654. On the whole, it was mainly in the second half of the century that French works spread over Europe. Naturally, the problem differed as between countries like England and Germany, where Protestantism prevailed, and those like Spain and Italy, where Catholicism was dominant.

After the exceptionally brilliant period of the sixteenth century, Spain lost its creative importance. She still produced ecstatics, of whom the best known is the Franciscan nun, Maria d'Agreda (1602–65): the revelations—rather surprising, one must admit—contained in her posthumous work *The Mystical City of God* (1670) excited fierce controversy and provided arguments for the anti-mystics. But the Iberian peninsula at that time produced mainly theologians, who set themselves to construct vast syntheses of mystical theology, carefully stripped of the Neoplatonic audacities of the Northern school, which had been acclimatized by St John of the Cross. They, too, interpolated and corrected the saint's work, to make it conform to their system. Their huge and somewhat forbidding Latin treatises did not reach the general public, but their influence on professional theologians long continued. And so some of their names deserve to be remembered, such as Agustin Antolinez (1554–1626), or the Carmelites Thomas of Jesus (1564–1627) and Joseph of the Holy Spirit (1667–1736).

Italy continued to be a very active centre of spirituality. Up to the Quietist crisis mysticism developed there freely enough, but without producing any really important work. The very remarkable works of Cardinal Bona (1609–74), a great admirer of Malaval, are in fact chiefly ascetical. But many French authors were translated there, in particular St Francis de Sales, Canfield, Bernières, Surin, Pierre de Poitiers, Malaval and Mme Guyon, a perilous privilege which, as we have seen, caused several of them to be put on the Index at the time of Quietism. But in Italy mysticism recovered sooner than in France, and in the eighteenth century there were some timid but very interesting attempts. The copious theoretical work of the Jesuit Giovanni Battista Scaramelli (1687–1752) was for long a classic, and inspired numerous successors, in spite of its heaviness and artificiality, partly due to the influence of Alvarez de Paz. Similarly, the countless spiritual writings of St Alphonsus de Liguori (1696–1787) had a lasting popularity, though they were of very unequal value. St Alphonsus was himself a very great mystic, and it is a pity we possess no analysis of his interior states. In contrast, St Paul of the Cross (1694–1775), the founder of the Passionists, has left us some heart-rending fragments of a spiritual diary, relating the terrible passive trials through which he had to pass.

In Germany conditions were different, because of the prevalence of Lutheranism. By the force of circumstances Catholics there were kept rather on the fringe of the movement which appeared in the Latin countries. But there was profound sympathy for mysticism and the writings of the Rheno-Flemish school were still read. In proof of this could be cited the Latin work of the Jesuit Maximilian Sandaeus (1578–1656), author of a very remarkable *Mystical Theology* (1627) and chiefly famed for his *Key to Mystical Theology* (1640). It is an interesting attempt at a reasoned vocabulary, in which nearly all the material is drawn from the Northern school, St Teresa and St John of the Cross being scarcely quoted. Official Lutheranism was very reserved on these matters, but many sects caused their adherents to live in an ardent interior tension, and some powerful personalities emerged. Beginning with Weigel and Boehme in the sixteenth century, the movement continued in the seventeenth with Frankenberg and Spener. It gave Catholic mysticism one of its most interesting writers in the person of the convert Johann Scheffler (1624–77): in 1657, under the pseudonym of Angelus Silesius, Scheffler produced his admirable *Cherubic pilgrim,* in which through many intermediaries, the grand tradition springing from Master Eckhart was still further prolonged. Then of course Germany was comparatively little affected by the Quietist crisis, and mysticism there went freely on its way.

In England, the condition of Catholicism was too precarious to allow any works of great value to be produced; the only exception is the Benedictine, Dom Augustine Baker (1575–1641). On becoming a Catholic he joined the Benedictines at Padua (1605) and was ordained priest some ten years later. He was for a time at Douai and Cambrai where he was the director of Dame Gertrude More (1606–33) whose life he wrote. His principal claim to fame is his *Sancta Sophia, or Holy Wisdom,* a posthumous work, of Dionysian tendency, very much in the tradition of the fourteenth-century English mystics.

Within Anglicanism there appeared an evolution towards a subjective and interior piety of a directly mystical type, as seen in the lovely poems of Henry Vaughan (1622–95). The tendency increased during the century in Anglican circles, where a whole group entered into relations with Fénelon and Mme Guyon, and the curious figure of the Chevalier Ramsay appeared. The movement eventually flowered in the founder of Methodism, John Wesley (1703–91), whose spiritual anthologies award a high place to the Catholic mystics. Similar tendencies appeared in French-speaking Calvinist circles, especially in connection with Pastor Pierre Poiret (1646–1719), friend and publisher of Mme Guyon, and with his successor Jean-Philippe Dutoit (1721–93). In this respect it is certain that Protestant circles did much to prepare for the revival of mystical piety which took place in the nineteenth century.

SELECT BIBLIOGRAPHY

AUCLAIR, Marcelle: *Saint Teresa of Avila*, London, Burns Oates, and New York, Pantheon, 1953.

BAKER, Augustine, O.S.B.: *Sancta Sophia*, London, Burns Oates, 1905.

BEDOYERE, Michael de la: *The Archbishop and the Lady*, London, Collins, 1956.

BREMOND, Henri: *Literary History of Religious Thought in France*, 3 Volumes, London, S.P.C.K., and New York, Macmillan, 1929–37.

BRODRICK, James, S.J.: *St Ignatius Loyola: The Pilgrim Years*, London, Burns Oates, and New York, Farrar, Straus, 1956; *Origin of the Jesuits*, London and New York, Longmans, 1940; *Progress of the Jesuits*, London and New York, Longmans, 1947.

BRUNO DE JÉSUS-MARIE, O.C.D.: *St John of the Cross*, London and New York, Sheed and Ward, 1936.

CALVET, J.: *Saint Vincent de Paul*, translated by Lancelot C. Sheppard, London, Burns Oates, and New York, McKay, 1952.

GARRIGOU-LAGRANGE, Reginald, O.P.: *The Three Ages of the Interior Life*, St Louis, Herder, 1947.

IGNATIUS OF LOYOLA, St: *Spiritual Exercises*, translated by Louis J. Puhl, Westminster, Md, Newman Press, 1951; *Text of the Spiritual Exercises*, translated from the original Spanish, London, Burns Oates, 1929.

JOHN OF THE CROSS, St: *The Complete Works of St John of the Cross*, translated and edited by E. Allison Peers from the Critical Edition of P. Silverio de Santa Teresa, C.D., 3 Volumes, London, Burns Oates, and Westminster, Md, Newman Press, 1953.

KNOX, R. A.: *Enthusiasm*, Oxford and New York, Oxford Univ. Press, 1950.

PARENTE, Pascal: *The Mystical Life*, St Louis, Herder, 1946; *The Ascetical Life*, St Louis, Herder, 1955.